Praise for Ani Phyo

"Ani's food is. . .inspiring. This book. . .
makes raw cuisine accessible for everyone to enjoy."
—Juliano Brotman, author of *Raw: The Uncookbook*

"Her array of delicious recipes will convince you that eating raw is not impossible
and definitely not boring."
—*Curve*

"As an actress, athlete, and American Gladiator,
I am always aware of what foods I eat to fuel my performance and keep my body
healthy. Ani's book gives the gft of wonderful desserts that are actually good for
you, utilizing nutrients that we may not get elsewhere that promote longevity,
beauty, healthy blood sugar levels and weight management!"
—Robin "Hellga" Coleman

"*Ani's Raw Food Desserts* is a lovely addition to any home and kitchen. By using the
delicious, easy to make, recipes in this book you will learn how and why raw food
is the coolest trend to emerge out of California since surfing."
—David Wolfe, author of *Naked Chocolate*

"Reading *Ani's Raw Food Kitchen* is a must if you want to treat your body with first
class nutrition and your mind with first class advice."
—Howard F. Lyman, author of *Mad Cowboy*

Ani's
Raw Food

Desserts

. . . .

85 *Easy, Delectable Sweets and Treats*

. . . .

Ani Phyo

Da Capo
∞
LIFE
LONG

**A MEMBER OF
THE PERSEUS BOOKS GROUP**

This book is dedicated to you, the reader, for choosing to strive for optimal health, radiance, and beauty for yourself and our planet. Thanks for sharing in my vision for a green, healthy planet filled with healthy, vibrant, happy, beautiful, kind, and loving people. Beauty has no boundaries, it's a gift we can share with everyone.

Copyright © 2009 by Ani Phyo
Food photographs, cover photograph, headshot Copyright © 2009 by Seth Beck
Ingredient photographs Copyright © 2009 by Duc Nguyen
Illustrations Copyright © 2009 by Antonio Sanchez

Designed by Pauline Neuwirth, Neuwirth & Associates, Inc.
Set in 9-point Scala Sans by the Perseus Books Group

Cataloging-in-Publication data for this book is available from the Library of Congress.

First Da Capo Press edition 2009
ISBN: 978-0-7382-1306-4

Published by Da Capo Press
A Member of the Perseus Books Group
www.dacapopress.com

Note: The information in this book is true and complete to the best of our knowledge. This book is intended only as an informative guide for those wishing to know more about health issues. In no way is this book intended to replace, countermand, or conflict with the advice given to you by your own physician. The ultimate decision concerning care should be made between you and your doctor. We strongly recommend you follow his or her advice. Information in this book is general and is offered with no guarantees on the part of the authors or Da Capo Press. The authors and publisher disclaim all liability in connection with the use of this book. The names and identifying details of people associated with events described in this book have been changed. Any similarity to actual persons is coincidental.

Da Capo Press books are available at special discounts for bulk purchases in the United States by corporations, institutions, and other organizations. For more information, please contact the Special Markets Department at the Perseus Books Group, 2300 Chestnut Street, Suite 200, Philadelphia, PA, 19103, or call (800) 810-4145, ext. 5000, or e-mail special.markets@perseusbooks.com.

10 9 8 7 6 5 4 3 2 1

Contents

Introduction

Sweet Inspirations

THE MOUTH-WATERING desserts in this book provide healthy, whole food nutrition you can include in any diet as a meal, snack, or dessert. The treats are so tasty, you won't miss the wheat, gluten, sugar, and dairy—or the guilt!

This way of eating isn't just another diet. It's a lifestyle shift toward better health. Eating more of my desserts will help you become healthier. You'll be forgoing a traditional slice of cake made of flour, sugar, eggs, butter, and trans fat for one made with delicious nuts and fruit. You can't go wrong.

But there's no need to be extreme, this isn't an all-or-nothing deal. I'm simply offering options for you as you wind your way along your path toward greater health and vitality. You'll see benefits from adding any of my treats to your existing diet. Most of my recipes take less time to put together than traditional recipes and don't require heating or baking, which means less time in the kitchen . . . a bonus for us busy folks. Plus, my desserts will make you lean, strong, happy, healthy, and beautiful—from the inside out.

The recipes in the Sun-Baked Treats chapter are fun for adding another texture: crunch. Dehydrating is the raw food way of baking at low temperatures. These recipes won't take much more prep or cleanup time, just more patience as it can be hours before you can enjoy them.

What Is Raw Food?

RAW LIVING FOODS are foods made using fresh, unheated raw fruits, vegetables, nuts, and seeds. We eat this way to achieve ultimate health, vitality, and beauty; to maintain a healthy weight; to avoid food allergens like wheat, dairy, and gluten; and because it's outright delicious!

Raw fresh fruits, vegetables, nuts, and seeds are full of living enzymes and vital nutrients like vitamins, minerals, amino acids, and water. Eating food unheated and fresh, the way Mother Earth intended, makes it easier for our bodies to digest. This lessens overall stress on our bodies and leaves us with excess energy to fuel our peak physical and mental performance. Eating fresh and raw also boosts our immune systems and keeps us healthy and strong. The healthier we are, the better we feel and look, and the slower we age. A strong, vibrantly healthy body on the inside shows up on the surface as the healthy glow of clear, radiant skin coupled with increased overall well-being.

Delicious sweet treats and desserts got me hooked on raw living foods. It was easy to choose healthy, cruelty-free, decadent desserts over those filled with allergens and refined sugar and laden with guilt. I used to run for an hour just to make myself feel better about having eaten a bad-for-me dessert. Now, I enjoy my delicious, nutritious, whole food desserts on their own as a healthy meal!

I've also included a chapter on treats made with wine and champagne. Depending on where you sit on the continuum, you may feel a glass of wine—or some fruit soaked in wine—is good for you, providing antioxidants and supporting heart health. Or, you may choose to abstain from alcohol altogether. I choose moderation. Feel free to tailor the recipes to suit your needs.

Be Green, Lean, and Serene

You'll be doing your part in contributing to the future of our planet by making and enjoying my recipes. As you eat more whole fresh ingredients, you'll notice your body becoming leaner and healthier, plus your lifestyle will shift closer to the sustainability and green living end of the continuum. Here's how this happens:

First, you'll notice a decrease in garbage in your kitchen. I'll make treats for 50, and be left only with organic compost and recycling. Buy in bulk when possible and you'll be surprised at how much waste processed food packaging creates. And remember, it's always better to reuse than to recycle since recycling requires resources like shipping and manufacturing.

Second, buying local and seasonal means your food travels less, is fresher, and is less vulnerable to food contamination along the way. Food travels between 1,400 and 2,500 miles from farm to table, so you can bet the huge amounts of fuel used to transport our food contributes to global warming. Shop as locally and as seasonally as possible by visiting your neighborhood farmers' market. Fruits and vegetables taste the best and offer the highest nutrient values when in season.

Third, my food is cruelty-free and our animal friends are unharmed, leaving natural resources intact. *Environmental Science and Technology* reports that eating less red meat and dairy is an even more effective way of lowering the average U.S. household's food-related climate footprint than buying local food. Yes, switching to a totally local diet saves about 1,000 miles of driving per year, but replacing red meat and dairy with vegetables just one day per week saves resources equal to 1,160 miles of driving per year. Switching to a completely vegan diet is the equivalent to driving 8,100 fewer miles per year.

Fourth, by choosing organic when possible, you're limiting the food toxins and chemicals in your body. You're also helping eliminate synthetic pesticides, chemicals, and genetic modifications and their contamination to farmers, land, our food sources, and our drinking water. Organic food also eliminates the production of these chemicals, along with machinery and packaging, which decreases greenhouse gases in our atmosphere.

Fifth, cooking and baking at home and in commercial bakeries and factories uses more energy than we realize. So does manufacturing and transporting large stoves and ovens. I'm not asking you to get rid of your stove, but making these sweet treats will help you be aware of your stove's carbon footprint.

Finally, your body will thank you. You'll feel stronger, healthier, and more vibrant on the inside. Radiant health, clear skin, shiny hair, and a powerful, lean, and beautiful body is what shows up on the outside.

Raw Desserts: Good, and Good for You

My desserts are made with fresh, nutritious ingredients that help contribute to your overall health and well-being. Fresh fruits, vegeta-bles, nuts, and seeds provide anti-aging minerals, vitamins, and phytochemicals for radiant clear skin, strong nails and hair, bright eyes, and a healthy glow. These are the nutrients that'll keep us looking and feeling youthful by slowing down our overall aging process, keeping our brains sharp, and keeping our bodies agile, graceful, and strong.

My recipes help you eat more of the following beautifying, slimming, and strengthening nutrients:

ANTI-AGING ANTIOXIDANTS

Free radicals are not our friends. Formed from sun exposure, pollution, and stress, they cause oxidation "rusting" of cells, speed up aging, and cause premature wrinkling of skin, muscles, and brain. **Antioxidants** can rescue us from free-radical, age-accelerating damage. Colorful fruits and vegetables like berries, citrus, melon, stone fruit, corn, and peppers are packed with powerful anti-aging antioxidants like vitamins A, C, and E, along with zinc, iron, and selenium.

VITAMINS

VITAMINS A, C, AND E work together to build the collagen that keeps skin firm. They protect us from wrinkles and fine lines, sun exposure, and ultraviolet light damage. These vitamins are necessary for the maintenance and repair of skin tissue and keep our skin smooth and youthful. Age-defying nuts and seeds, like cashews, almonds, walnuts, and flax and hemp seeds, are packed with vitamin E. Research on study participants over 65 years old found the most agile people with the highest physical performance measured by speed, coordination, and balance had adequate amounts of vitamin E in their system.

B-VITAMINS, including B_1 (thiamin), B_3 (niacin), B_5 (pantothenic acid), and B_7 (biotin), form the basis of skin, nail, and hair cells and strengthen cardiovascular health and blood flow for glowing, healthy skin. Found in fruits like peaches, bananas, melon, and strawberries, they keep skin hydrated and moisturized to appear plumper, healthier, and younger. Essential for skin and hair growth, B-vitamins also help prevent hair loss.

MINERALS
SELENIUM, COPPER, AND ZINC, to name a few minerals, play key roles in skin cancer prevention, protecting our skin from sun damage and burning. Minerals also help skin develop elastin, the fibers supporting the skin's structure from underneath, for firmer, more youthful skin. Acne can be a symptom of zinc deficiency.

To get more minerals, enjoy fruits like blackberries, limes, strawberries, lemons, melon, and bananas.

ESSENTIAL FATTY ACIDS
EFAS are crucial for growing healthy skin, hair, and nails. They improve overall complexion through internal hydration. Studies show two key fatty acids, omega-3 and omega-6, reduce inflammation and wrinkles, improve skin tone, keep skin looking smoother and younger, and regulate body weight. Plus, omega-3 fatty acids lower cholesterol and lift your mood. Nuts and seeds of all types are great sources of EFAs.

HEALTHY FATS
COCONUT OIL is said to be nature's perfect food. It contains lauric acid, a special kind of saturated fat found to speed up weight loss. It reduces the risk of heart disease, high blood pressure, and many other health problems. Studies have found coconut oil

stimulates thyroid function and has antiseptic and anti-aging properties.

OLIVE OIL is high in antioxidants and includes vitamin E's anti-aging protection.

HEMP AND FLAXSEED AND OILS balance dry skin, fight skin inflammations, offer anti-aging and moisture-balancing properties, and provide omega EFAs.

NUTS AND SEEDS combat wrinkles, stop skin from sagging, keep skin looking younger, and also reduce our risk of heart disease, cancer, and diabetes. They also help with weight control.

PROTEIN
PROTEIN from nuts and seeds helps repair the cells of hair, skin, and nails (which are mostly made of protein).

Ingredients
I love spending time in the kitchen and entertaining, but my life has grown busier with lots of travel and less time for making complex meals for friends. For the sake of time, my recipes have become more simple. This has allowed me to discover the power of using fewer ingredients and letting each unique flavor really come through. Most of my recipes use only a few ingredients placed in the food processor or blender to whip up quickly and then enjoy. This is how I eat every day at home and on the road. Simple, fast, and easy.

My recipes include antioxidant-rich, nutrient-dense, organic fruits, nuts, and seeds. These are all technically superfoods and are easy to find in grocery stores and natural food stores. Additional superfoods like goji berries, maca, flax, hemp, chia, and coconut can be more difficult to find but will add powerful nutrients to your diet.

Look for organic ingredients online, including my website and online store at *www.AniPhyo.com*.

FRUITS

I prefer using fresh, local, seasonal fruit whenever possible. In warmer months, I love to visit my local farmers' market for the freshest, tastiest, and most nutritious fruits and veggies. If you're unable to make it to a market, don't have fresh foods available where you are, or are on a time crunch, you can use frozen fruits in my recipes. But, you can't beat fresh. It'll always look and taste best.

NUTS AND SEEDS

Look for raw and choose organic nuts and seeds whenever possible.

SOAKING NUTS AND SEEDS: Ideally, all nuts and seeds should first be soaked overnight and rinsed well before using for optimal nutritional value. I don't pretend to be perfect and occasionally you'll find me eating unsoaked nuts, especially when I'm on the road. Do what works for you. Unsoaked raw nuts and seeds work and taste fine in my recipes, too.

DRYING NUTS AND SEEDS: Some of my recipes call for "dry" nuts or seeds. To dry soaked nuts and seeds, place them in the sun on a tray or in your dehydrator at 104°F for 4 to 6 hours. Or, just use nuts and seeds that have not been soaked.

ALMOND MEAL

You can buy almond meal or make your own by grinding dried almonds into a fine powder. Almond meal will give your recipe a flour flavor and texture, without the gluten that'll make you puffy and bloated.

OTHER SUPERFOODS

Most of my recipes use common, easy-to-find ingredients. I've added a couple bonus recipes that use harder-to-find superfood ingredients, which you can order online, or substitute with other more common foods. I wanted to take this opportunity to talk about these powerful functional foods so you can decide if you'd like to give them a try.

Superfoods give us the densest source of nutrients to supplement all diets. It's important to find good sources for harder-to-find organic superfood ingredients. One of my favorites is *Navitas Naturals*. It is a wonderful source for the highest-quality, tastiest super-foods I've found. For more information, visit *www.navitasnaturals.com*. I love all of Navitas Natural's products—here are a few of the ones I use in this book.

Cacao Beans, Nibs, and Powder

Cacao beans are the source for all cocoa and chocolate products. The beans come from a fruit that grows on trees in Central and South America. The nibs come from cracking open whole cacao beans; the powder is ground, fat-reduced cacao. These various forms are great for adding different textures to desserts.

Flaxseed and Powder

Flax is high in omega-3 fatty acid, fiber, and the antioxidant lignan. It's known to lower cholesterol and blood pressure. Flax's ability to hold water will keep you well hydrated. As with all nuts and seeds, it's best soaked overnight and rinsed to increase enzymes, amino acids, and vitamins while maximizing the body's ability to digest and absorb the nutritional benefits. It's a pain to soak, dry, and then grind flaxseed. It gets gelatinous when soaked, and if I'm going to dehydrate it, I'd rather eat it as a cracker. *Navitas Naturals* offers a convenient presprouted and ground flax powder for lazy folks like me. It's a staple in my kitchen.

Chia Seed and Powder

Chia is the Aztec superfood, eaten for strength and energy. Chia's ability to hold water will keep you hydrated and helps athletes retain electrolytes naturally. As with all nuts and seeds, it's best soaked overnight and rinsed to increase enzymes, amino acids, and vitamins while maximizing the body's ability to digest and absorb the nutritional benefits. As with flaxseed, chia is a bit of a process to soak, dry, and grind. So, I use a convenient presprouted and ground chia powder from *Navitas Naturals*.

Goji Berries

Known as the fruit of longevity and well-being, these red berries grow on vines in China. A complete protein, goji berries are loaded with 18 amino acids and all 8 essential amino acids. They contain more beta-carotene than carrots, more vitamin C than oranges, and more iron than steak. They also contain zinc, copper, phosphorus, vitamin E, and B complex vitamins. Goji berries have been used for 6,000 years by herbalists in China, Tibet, and India to boost immune function, strengthen the legs, improve circulation, and improve sexual function and fertility.

Maca Powder

Known as an adaptogen for its ability to increase the body's resistance to stress, anxiety, and fatigue, this Peruvian root restores our aging hormonal system back to that of its younger years by strengthening and toning our entire endocrine system. It promotes greater energy and stamina and rebuilds our adrenal glands. I use maca with cacao to offset the negative effects of the caffeine in chocolate.

Mesquite Powder

From ground pods of the mesquite tree, mesquite powder contains amino acids, calcium, magnesium, potassium, iron, and zinc. It also has fructose, which doesn't require insulin to digest, preventing spikes in blood sugar levels. It contributes great flavor and is a natural sweetener, especially when used with chocolate.

Mulberries, Dried

I've recently discovered mulberries, they're a new favorite. High in antioxidants, vitamin C, iron, and protein, the berry is made up of a cluster of tiny, closely packed mini berries, each of which contains a seed. The dried fruit has a sweet taste and slightly crunchy texture from the seeds.

Coconut Oil, Coconut Butter

Coconut oil and coconut butter are one and the same thing. Coconut is known to support thyroid function, is heart healthy, improves digestion, protects us from free-radical damage, and makes us look and feel younger. It is high in vitamin E, antioxidants, and the "good" fat, lauric acid, which the body burns off rather than storing as fat.

Most of my recipes call for liquid coconut oil. If solid, simply place the jar in a bowl of warm water and wait a few minutes. Then, pour off the liquid to use in the recipes.

Hemp Nut, Hemp Seed

The seed and nut are names for the same thing. Hemp is 33 percent protein, rich in antioxidants like chlorophyll and vitamin E, high in iron and essential fatty acids such as omega 3, 6, and 9, and builds strong, healthy hair, nails, and skin.

Hemp is literally a weed, has no natural pests, and grows easily anywhere. By growing

hemp, we help to restore soil, conserve forests, and contribute to a healthy green planet. In addition to being great for our diets, hemp is used to make paper, fabric, soaps, beauty products, and even shoes.

Nutiva is the brand I use for coconut oil and hemp products. The full character, fresh coconut flavor, and sweet coconut aroma is retained in Nutiva's coconut oil. Their hemp nuts are super fresh and of the highest quality I've found. For more information, visit *www.nutiva.com*.

Acai

Acai, an incredible palmberry from the Amazon rain forest, is packed with nutrients and considered one of the healthiest fruits. This superfood is packed with more antioxidants than blueberries or pomegranates, plus essential omegas, amino acids, and fiber.

Sambazon Pure Acai is palmberry pulp frozen within two days of picking and packaged into individual serving-sized packets. Sambazon preserves rain forests in Brazil from being cut down for lumber and creates fair trade and humane working conditions for farmers. For more information, visit *www.sambazon.com.*

WATER

Use filtered water instead of tap water whenever possible. Water filters help us to protect our bodies from over 2,100 known toxins that may be present in tap water. Filters remove chlorine and bacterial contaminants for better tasting and smelling water. They protect our bodies from disease and create overall greater health. Point-of-use water filters cost less than bottled water and help us keep awful plastic bottles out of our landfills.

SUBSTITUTIONS

Lately I've found myself using more short-cuts, including using easier ingredients, to speed up my food prep time. Feel free to adapt any of my recipes to best suit your needs. Here are some examples of how you might substitute some ingredients.

Sweeteners

The best way to sweeten is always with whole fruits like raisins, dates, figs, and prunes. For convenience, or to achieve a specific flavor profile, color, or texture, I'll use agave syrup or yacon syrup. Feel free to substitute agave syrup, yacon syrup, or maple syrup 1 to 1 in any recipe.

AGAVE NECTAR AND SYRUP: Both *nectar* and *syrup* refer to the same low-glycemic sweetener. I've recently begun using agave more for convenience and will use it in recipes when I'm going for a lighter color or texture.

YACON SYRUP: A low-glycemic, low-calorie sweetener, yacon syrup tastes a lot like molasses and caramel with less than half the sugar of agave syrup and a third of the calories per tablespoon. It's a recent discovery for me and a new favorite I use like any other sweetener for body and rich flavor. I use yacon syrup from *Navitas Naturals.* For more information on yacon syrup, visit *www.AniPhyo.com.*

MAPLE SYRUP: If you decide to use maple syrup, choose the darker, less filtered grade B, which has more minerals and is less processed than grade A.

Vanilla

For speed and ease, I'll use an alcohol-free vanilla extract over fresh vanilla bean. You can substitute:

Seeds from 1 vanilla bean = 1 tablespoon vanilla extract

To de-seed a vanilla bean, cut the bean the long way, then run a spoon along the open edge to catch the seeds. Use the seed pod in your blender to add vanilla flavor to smoothies and puddings. You can watch a video of me de-seeding a vanilla bean at *www.AniPhyo.com*.

Mint and Spices

In general, you can substitute half the amount of dried mint or spice for the amount I use fresh in my recipe.

Substitute 1 tablespoon chopped fresh mint with:

1½ teaspoons dried mint
1½ teaspoons dried mint from herbal mint teabag
½ teaspoon mint extract
1 drop peppermint oil

Nuts

Many of the recipes in this book use nuts and seeds. If you have a nut allergy or want to cut back on nuts, try substituting a vegetable pulp like carrot pulp when making a cake or cookie. Ideally, it's best to dry the pulp first by placing it in a dehydrator for 4 to 6 hours at 104°F. But if you don't have time, just use the fresh pulp to substitute the nuts 1 to 1. Depending on your desired consistency, you may need to use up to twice as much pulp as nuts.

Equipment and Tools

I'm a kitchen gadget freak and get to play with many of my favorite kitchen tools in this book. Most are fun to have, but not required. I use icons for different tools next to each recipe so you can see what you'll need at a glance. The tool to ideally have in your kitchen first is the Personal Blender, though a

to blend small batches, yet large enough to make several servings. It comes with three different blending cups (1-cup, 2-cup, and 3-cup), a blending lid, a grinding lid, and storing lids so you can blend, cover, and store all in one container. It even comes with a travel lid so you can take your smoothie to go! For those of us who prefer using glass, there's an attachment for blending with a mason jar. I use my Personal Blender daily, it's replaced my larger blenders. A must-have. For more information, visit *www.personalblender.com*.

HIGH-SPEED BLENDER

I have a more powerful high-speed blender for making larger batches and for blending thicker mixtures. Popular brands are Vita-Mix and K-Tec Champ. Both are expensive but will last a lifetime. My Vita-Mix blenders pulverize ingredients, have made food for thousands of folks, and are still going strong. Feel free to use a regular blender for now if that's what you've got. It's helpful to first use a grinder to grind up ingredients, like nuts, that would otherwise not break down well in a less powerful blender.

regular blender works fine too. The next tool is a food processor.

PERSONAL BLENDER

You can't beat the Personal Blender, my new favorite home blender from the Tribest Corporation. It's a small, travel-sized blender and grinder that's very reasonable in price. It's compact, making it easy

Food Processor

 After a Personal Blender or high-speed blender, the second piece of equipment for your kitchen is a food processor. Start with one with a 7-cup bowl. It will save you time chopping and mixing dry ingredients. But if you don't have one, you can always chop and mix the old-fashioned way, by hand.

Grinder

For processing nuts and seeds into a fine powder, you'll need some kind of grinder. You can use the Personal Blender, which comes with a grinder attachment. A coffee grinder works, too.

The Basics

 Mixing bowls, knives, cutting board, mixing spoon, and spatula.

More Fun Tools

Here are more tools that are fun to have, but not required.

A **CITRUS JUICER** will save you time and help you efficiently extract all the juice from a lemon or lime.

A **CITRUS ZESTER** is a fun tool for removing long strips of zest from lemons, limes, and oranges to use as pretty garnishes.

COOKIE CUTTERS are used for pressing dough into fun shapes.

An **ICE CREAM SCOOPER** makes it easy to portion and serve ice kreams, doughs, and batters. I have scoopers in 1-, 1½-, and 2-tablespoon sizes.

An **ICE CREAM MAKER** is useful for making frozen sorbets, ice kreams, and gelatos.

A **METAL CHOCOLATE MOLD TRAY** is used to make filled chocolates in beautiful shapes. The metal holds the cold so liquid chocolate solidifies right away.

A **SIEVE OR WIRE MESH STRAINER** is used for draining soaked and washed ingredients.

A **MELON BALLER** scoops melon into small ball shapes that are fun to eat.

A **VEGETABLE JUICER** creates carrot pulp as a by-product of carrot juice. You can also get pulp from a juice bar.

A **WIRE WHISK** will help you mix smoothly, without lumps.

Pans

Pans are convenient to have. But, if you don't have a pan, be creative and use any bowl or storage container that'll hold all your ingredients.

Springform cheesecake pan
Loaf pan
Small tartlet or brioche tins
Sheet tray
Pie dish

Muffin pan

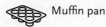 Cupcake liners

Tartlet pans

* * *

Dehydrator

Dehydrators dry food at low temperatures, like the sun. They come in round or square shapes from various manufacturers. Any type will work, though one with removable shelves for greater height between shelves will allow cupcakes and taller foods to fit. In the summertime, you can place food in the sun to dry naturally. Or, you can use your oven on the lowest temperature to dry food, opening the door or turning the heat on and off to

prevent overheating and baking the food. You'll see that the oven is the least energy-efficient way to dry and may decide to invest in a dehydrator when you can.

Teflex and ParaFlexx Sheets

Both are flexible, solid, nonstick reusable sheets for dehydrator trays. Teflex sheets are coated with Teflon, while ParaFlexx sheets are coated with silicone. You can use parchment paper if you don't have Teflex or ParaFlexx sheets.

No Equipment Necessary

Some recipes need nothing more than your own two hands. The hand icon means no heavy lifting and no equipment is needed to make the recipe.

At-a-Glance

THROUGHOUT THE BOOK I have three types of sidebars with handy icons to help you identify them:

SKINCARE AND BEAUTY

GREEN LIVING

OTHER TIPS AND INFORMATION TO HELP YOU LIVE A HEALTHIER, GREENER LIFE

1

Frozen Treats

CE CREAM DOESN'T have to be full of hard-to-digest and less-than-healthy sugar, dairy, and eggs in order to be tasty. In fact, the ingredients in these frozen treats are nutrient-rich, like nuts and seeds that provide protein, essential fatty acids, and minerals to keep us strong and fit, and our skin firm, moist, and smooth. Nuts are simply blended smooth to make a rich nut cream, then frozen in the same manner you'd make traditional dairy ice cream. Full of fruits for color and flavor, they're packed with powerful vitamins and antioxidants known to combat and even reverse aging. You won't miss the dairy once you've tried my chocolate dipped Bonbons, a decadent Ice Kream Sandwich, or creamy rich Coconut Ice Kream.

These frozen desserts will keep for a month or more in the freezer. So, keep your freezer stocked with my goodies and you'll always have delicious healthy treats to grab when your sweet tooth attacks.

Pineapple Icebox Dessert

MAKES 6 TO 8 SERVINGS

I have fond childhood summertime memories of eating pineapple icebox cake with my mother under our lilac tree, my favorite flower. Pineapple is full of the enzyme bromelaine, which helps decrease inflammation and swelling—that translates to increased circulation and clear skin. I always choose fresh when available, but frozen pineapple will also work for this recipe.

CRUST

2 cups cashews
Seeds from 1 vanilla bean, or 1 table-
    spoon alcohol-free vanilla extract
2 tablespoons agave syrup

FILLING

1½ cups cashews
⅓ cup agave syrup
¼ cup liquid coconut oil
¼ cup filtered water, as needed
2½ cups chopped cored pineapple

To make the crust, combine the cashews and vanilla in the food processor and chop to a crushed wafer texture. Add the agave syrup and process to mix well. Sprinkle half of the crust onto the bottom of a loaf pan.

To make the filling, combine the cashews, agave syrup, and coconut oil in the high-speed blender and blend until smooth, adding water as needed to create a creamy texture. Spoon the mixture into a mixing bowl, add the pineapple, and stir to mix well. Spoon the filling into the loaf pan and sprinkle the remaining crust on top. Pat lightly. Freeze for 2 hours, or until chilled.

Will keep for 4 to 6 days in fridge or for a several weeks in the freezer

Key Lime Kream Bars

The heat of the days in Baja on the Pacific inspired this rich, tart, creamy frozen treat. Just blend, pour, freeze, and enjoy! Citrus fruits of all types are packed with vitamin C and anti-aging properties.

4 cups cashews
1 cup lime juice
½ cup agave syrup
½ cup liquid coconut oil
1 cup filtered water, as needed

Combine the cashews, lime juice, agave syrup, and coconut oil in the high-speed blender and blend until smooth, adding water as needed. Scoop the mixture into a pie dish. Freeze until chilled, 2 to 3 hours. Cut into bars to serve.

Will keep for weeks in the freezer.

Ice Kream Sandwiches

MAKES 3 OR 4 SANDWICHES

My love for finger foods led me to create this handheld frozen treat. Tart, rich, smooth ice kream is sandwiched between layers of dark carob goodness.

½ recipe **Key Lime Kream Bars** (page 25)
Carob Walnut Cookies (page 115)

Spread the Key Lime Kream mixture in a pie pan or loaf pan to desired thickness. Somewhere between 1 and 1½ inches works well. Freeze until solid, 2 to 3 hours.

Roll the cookie dough onto a sheet tray lined with parchment paper. A layer between ¼ and ½ inch thick works well. Place in the freezer until firm, about 30 minutes.

Remove the dough from the freezer and use the cookie cutter(s) to stamp out your favorite shapes in pairs. Keep these cookies in the freezer until ready to assemble.

Once the ice kream is solid, use the same cookie cutter(s) to stamp out shapes. Remove the cookies from the freezer and sandwich each ice kream shape between 2 cookies. Serve immediately, or store in freezer until ready.

Will keep in the freezer for several weeks or more.

VARIATIONS:
Try rolling the outside edge of the sandwiches in ¼ cup crushed nuts, dried fruit, cacao nibs, or another favorite topping. Use **Coconut Ice Kream** (page 35) or **Lemon Kreamsicles** (page 36) instead of the lime bars.

Bonbons

I got so excited when I discovered that my liquid chocolate magically freezes in seconds on my frozen ice kream, making a crunchy candy topping—just like at the soft-serve ice cream stand where cones are dipped upside down in a vat of liquid chocolate. This time the chocolate is a nutritious superfood and the ice kream is cruelty-free.

¼ recipe **Key Lime Kream Bars** (page 25), refrigerated
½ recipe **Liquid Chocolate** (page 74)

With a scooper or with your hands, make tablespoon-sized balls of the refrigerated **Key Lime Kream Bar** batter. Place the balls on parchment paper. Chill in the freezer for at least 1 hour.

Place the **Liquid Chocolate** in a small bowl or ramekin. Once the ice kream balls are frozen solid enough, use a spoon to dip each into the chocolate. Place on a sheet tray lined with parchment paper and serve, or cover and store in the freezer.

Will keep for several weeks in the freezer.

Chill Out

WE FEEL BETTER when we can relax and chill out more. Plus, we look less haggard and strung-out. One way I love to relax is in a candlelit hot lavender bath enjoying a frozen treat. It's especially fun to eat messier handhelds in the bathtub, like Bonbons, Ice Kream Sandwiches, and Sundae Cones. It's even more fun to share bath time with your special sweetie.

Mango Sorbet

This recipe calls for frozen mangoes, my favorite fruit. I always prefer fresh everything, so I'll prepare fresh mango a day or two before and then freeze it. Frozen mango from the freezer aisle will work, too.

2 cups chopped frozen mangoes
1 cup filtered water
⅓ cup agave syrup

Combine the mangoes, water, and agave syrup in the high-speed blender and blend until smooth. Serve immediately. Or, for an icier, more solid texture, scoop into a container and place in the freezer for an hour or more.

To make in an ice cream maker: Chill the mixture in the freezer for an hour or so, then scoop into the ice cream maker and follow the manufacturer's instructions.

Will keep for several weeks in freezer. Let thaw for 10 minutes before serving.

Apricot Basil Sorbet

MAKES 4 SERVINGS

The beta-carotene in an apricot is the phytonutrient responsible for its lovely orange color. Packed with vitamins C and A to slow down aging of our skin, apricots protect our eyes and heart. Basil is known to help protect DNA from radiation, is an anti-bacterial and anti-inflammatory, and is a good source of iron, calcium, and potassium.

5 cups frozen cubed pitted apricots
½ cup agave syrup
½ to ¾ cup apple juice or coconut
    water, as needed
1 tablespoon chopped fresh basil

Combine the apricots and agave syrup in the food processor and pulse into small pieces. Add ½ cup juice or water and mix until smooth, adding more liquid if needed. Add the basil and pulse to mix well. Enjoy immediately.

To make in an ice cream maker, scoop the mixture into the ice cream maker and follow manufacturer's instructions for a more solid texture

VARIATION:
Try substituting mint for the basil: 1 tablespoon chopped fresh mint, 1½ teaspoons dried mint, or ½ teaspoon mint extract.

ANI'S RAW FOOD DESSERTS

Vanilla Cacao Crunch Ice Mylk

Frozen cacao nibs give a great crispy crunch to light, icy, cashew kream kissed with vanilla. You can make this with or without an ice cream maker.

2 cups cashews
2 cups filtered water
⅓ cup agave syrup
2 tablespoons alcohol-free vanilla extract,
    or the seeds from 2 vanilla beans
¼ cup cacao nibs

Combine the cashews, water, and agave syrup in the high-speed blender and blend until smooth. Scoop the mixture into a container and top with the cacao nibs. Place in the freezer for 3 to 4 hours. Once it begins to freeze, remove every hour or so and stir, then place back in freezer; repeat until desired consistency.

To make in the ice cream maker: Chill the mixture in the freezer for an hour or two, then scoop into the ice cream maker and follow the manufacturer's instructions.

Best enjoyed immediately but will keep in freezer for several weeks.

VARIATIONS:

For mint chip, add in a few drops of peppermint oil. For chocolate ice mylk, add 1 to 2 tablespoons cacao powder. And for mint chocolate chip, add both.

Coconut Ice Kream

You can enjoy this smooth, creamy, coconut treat on its own, topped with your favorite syrup or fruit. You can simply freeze the kream without an ice cream maker because my ice kream won't freeze ice hard in the freezer. It has the same texture as traditional ice cream, minus the chemical emulsifiers and guar gums.

If you're lucky enough to find Thai baby coconuts, you can substitute 1 cup Thai coconut for the ¼ cup shredded coconut here and replace the filtered water with fresh coconut water.

1 cup cashews
1 cup filtered water
⅓ cup agave syrup
¼ cup shredded coconut
¼ cup liquid coconut oil

Combine the cashews, water, agave syrup, coconut, and oil in the high-speed blender and blend until smooth. Scoop the mixture into a container and place in the freezer for 3 to 4 hours. Every hour or so, remove and mix well. Place back in freezer to chill. Repeat until desired consistency, 5 to 7 hours.

To make in an ice cream maker: Chill the mixture in the freezer for hour or two, until cold. Scoop the chilled mixture into the ice cream maker and follow the manufacturer's instructions.

Will keep for several weeks in the freezer.

VARIATIONS:
Swirl in a sauce, like **Raspberry Sauce** (page 177) or **Chocolate Sauce** (page 178), as soon as the mixture begins to freeze. Or, try folding in fruit like blueberries or chopped strawberries.

Lemon Kreamsicles

MAKES 4 SERVINGS

These creamy, rich, lemon-banana popsicles are full of antioxidants, vitamin C, and potassium for warding off and reversing the signs of aging and sun damage. Fast and easy to make, popsicles are always fun to eat.

⅔ cup cashews
3 bananas
½ cup lemon juice (from 3 to 4 lemons)
¼ cup agave syrup

Combine all the ingredients in the high-speed blender and blend until smooth. Scoop the mixture into four ½-cup popsicle molds and place in the freezer for several hours, or until frozen.

Will keep for many weeks in the freezer.

Sundae Cones

This recipe was created for Seth Beck, who's been an amazing inspiration in my life. You are never going to believe these decadent sundaes are good for you.

Ice Kream Cones (page 163)
½ recipe **Liquid Chocolate** (page 74)
½ recipe **Key Lime Kream Bars** (page 25)
or 1 recipe **Coconut Ice Kream** (page 35) or 2 cups of your favorite sorbet
¼ cup crushed walnuts

Place each cone upright in a glass that won't crack in the freezer, like a thick rocks glass or a paper cup, and place in the freezer to chill for 15 to 30 minutes.

Remove the cold cones one at a time and drizzle each on the inside with 3 to 4 tablespoons of the **Liquid Chocolate** while rotating and keeping upright. Place back in freezer to harden the chocolate.

Remove the cones from the freezer and scoop ice kream or sorbet into each. Top with **Liquid Chocolate** and crushed nuts and serve immediately.

Sundae cones made with **Key Lime Kream** or **Coconut Ice Kream** will keep in the freezer for several weeks. Sundae cones made with sorbets will keep, too, but the sorbet will freeze solid and may be difficult to eat by hand.

Green Your Fridge

ABOUT 14 PERCENT of a typical household's electricity is used by the fridge. Here are a few simple changes to lighten your refrigerator's need for energy and its impact on our environment while decreasing toxic chemicals and bacteria.

CHOOSE GLASS

Glass keeps food and beverages colder, meaning less work for the fridge. We can see through glass, and chances are better that we'll see and eat our leftovers before they spoil. Glass doesn't leach chemicals like plastic does, so it's cleaner for our bodies, our home, and our planet.

KEEP A FULL, ORDERLY FRIDGE

A full fridge uses less energy than an empty one. If necessary, fill up empty shelves with tubs of water. Create a system of organization in your fridge to decrease time spent with the door open searching for things. Restaurants will put new stock at the back, and food that will spoil sooner in the front so it's used first.

MIND SPOILAGE

Pay attention to expiration, sell-by, and use-by dates on your food and toss leftovers after three or four days.

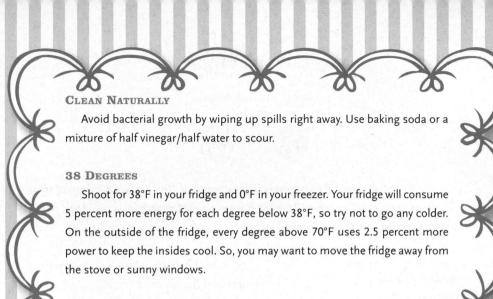

CLEAN NATURALLY

Avoid bacterial growth by wiping up spills right away. Use baking soda or a mixture of half vinegar/half water to scour.

38 DEGREES

Shoot for 38°F in your fridge and 0°F in your freezer. Your fridge will consume 5 percent more energy for each degree below 38°F, so try not to go any colder. On the outside of the fridge, every degree above 70°F uses 2.5 percent more power to keep the insides cool. So, you may want to move the fridge away from the stove or sunny windows.

SKIP ICE AND WATER DISPENSERS

Ice and water dispensers increase energy use by 14 to 20 percent, according to the U.S. Department of Energy.

GO TOP-HEAVY

A fridge with the freezer on top uses 10 to 25 percent less energy than side-by-side models. Opt for a smaller fridge that uses less energy and always look for the Energy Star label.

Cantaloupe Granita

A granitas is an easy and tasty treat for the summertime. This homemade slush or snow cone was the earliest form of ice cream. Typically granitas are made with fruit juices. In this recipe, I blend cantaloupe cubes for added fiber and body.

3 cups cubed cantaloupe
1 cup filtered water
⅓ cup agave syrup
¼ cup lemon juice

Combine all the ingredients in the high-speed blender and blend until smooth. Pour into a 13 by 9-inch baking pan and place in the freezer. Every 20 minutes, take the pan out and scrape the mixture with a fork to break apart the frozen pieces. Put back in freezer and repeat until all the liquid is frozen.

SERVING SUGGESTIONS:
Pour the granita mixture into fun popsicle molds and freeze. Or for snow cones or shaved ice, pour the mixture into ice trays and freeze, then process the cubes to small pieces in the food processor just before serving.

Ruby Grapefruit Granita

MAKES 4 SERVINGS

A citrus juicer will make this recipe fast and easy to make. The granita is bright in color, light, and refreshing and looks pretty served in wide-mouthed glasses topped with fresh sprigs of mint.

2½ cups fresh pink or ruby grapefruit
    juice, at room temperature
1 cup water
⅓ cup agave syrup
Fresh mint sprigs, for garnish

Combine the juice, water, and agave syrup in a bowl and stir to mix well. Pour into a 13 by 9-inch baking pan and freeze until hard, 3 to 4 hours.

To serve, scrape with a fork and spoon. Place scrapings into small martini glasses or small bowls. Garnish with sprigs of mint.

SERVING SUGGESTIONS:
Pour the granita mixture into fun popsicle molds. Or, for snow cones or shaved ice, pour the mixture into ice trays and freeze, then process the cubes to small pieces in the food processor just before serving.

Italian Ices with Lemon Syrup and Tutti Frutti Sauce

MAKES 4 SERVINGS

It takes only a few minutes to make this dessert of refreshing ice, tart lemon syrup, and a beautiful berry sauce. It's delicious and full of antioxidants and vitamin C to keep our summer skin looking youthful.

LEMON SYRUP
    4 lemons, zested and juiced
    ¼ cup agave syrup

TUTTI FRUTTI SAUCE
    1 cup strawberries
    ¼ cup agave syrup
    1 tablespoon alcohol-free vanilla extract,
        or the seeds from 1 vanilla bean
    ½ cup blackberries
    ½ cup raspberries

ITALIAN ICE
    4 cups ice

To make the lemon syrup, combine the lemon juice, zest, and agave syrup in a mixing bowl and mix well.

To make the tutti frutti sauce, combine the strawberries, agave syrup, and vanilla in the Personal Blender with the blending lid and 1-cup container. Gently pulse to a chunky texture. Spoon into a bowl and stir in the blackberries and raspberries.

To make the Italian ice, place the ice in the food processor and chop into tiny pieces.

Use an ice cream scooper to tightly pack and scoop the ice into 4 dishes. Top with lemon syrup first, then the tutti frutti sauce. Enjoy immediately.

Cherry Malt Chip Blizzards

MAKES 4 SERVINGS

This cherry bliss is kissed with crunchy cacao nibs, which taste so good and crunchy when they're cold.

4 cups frozen pitted cherries
¼ to ⅓ cup agave syrup, to taste
¼ cup carob powder
⅓ to ½ cup apple juice or coconut water, as needed
3 tablespoons cacao nibs

Combine the cherries, agave syrup, and carob powder in the food processor and pulse to break down the cherries. Next, add only enough juice or water to make a smooth texture. Add the cacao nibs and pulse a few times to mix. You don't want to break down the cacao nibs. Enjoy immediately.

To make in an ice cream maker: Scoop the mixture into the ice cream maker and follow manufacturer's instructions.

Will keep in the freezer for several weeks. It will freeze solid, so you'll want to let it thaw for 5 to 10 minutes, or even pulse in the food processor, before serving.

2

Cakes
and
Tartlets

RAW CAKES AND TARTLETS may not sound too appetizing, especially if you're picturing runny batters and uncooked dough. But . . . I promise these recipes will help you create the most delicious, decadent, and beautiful treats on the planet. Inspired by the cooked versions, they have been tested on kids and adults of all ages and have proven to be absolutely yummy.

The secret to my cakes is that they are made using chopped nuts that are bound together and naturally sweetened by sticky fruits, usually pitted dates. The texture is dense and similar to that of a flourless cake. The creamy parts, like frosting or a rich cheesecake filling, are made by blending nuts with fruits, chocolate, or spices for flavor.

These ingredients might sound weird to you at first, but give my Raspberry Ganache Fudge Cake, Lemon Pudding Filled Coconut Cupcakes with Shaved Coconut Topping, and Chocolate Crunch Cupcakes with Molten Mint Frosting a try, and you'll be hooked.

Naturally sweetened with whole fruit and packed with protein from nuts and seeds, my desserts help us build lean muscle and tissue while speeding up our metabolism and helping us lose weight! Enjoy nutrient-rich foods, and you'll notice you have less room for the empty foods, fillers, and bulk that make you fat. You'll be satisfied sooner and feel fuller longer.

Most of my cakes will keep for many weeks in the fridge or freezer. Make extra so you'll always have delicious, healthy, beautifying cakes on hand to enjoy for breakfast, lunch, and as a waist-whittling snack. Let there be cake!

Natural Cleansers

THE BEST NONTOXIC natural degreasers and cleansers can be found in our kitchens.

LEMONS

You'll notice that many regular cleaners include lemon for its fresh scent and degreasing power. For the same reasons, leftover lemon rinds work as a natural way for degreasing and cleaning. I use the rind like a sponge on my counters and in the bathroom. Try placing six to twelve lemon rinds in your bath, and fill with several inches of water. Leave overnight, then sponge away all the grime the next day.

Lemon juice is also a great surface cleaner and deodorizer. Mix lemon juice with salt to clean copper and brass. Leave half a lemon in the fridge to absorb smells and deodorize.

BAKING SODA

Baking soda is a great scrub for cleaning stainless steel, cast iron, and even nonstick surfaces. Add it to the dishwashing liquids and detergents to use less and mix it with vinegar to clean the shower glass doors.

COCONUT OIL

Coconut oil is a great household remover for the sticky glue residue leftover from price tags on glass or plastic and also works well as a natural eye makeup remover. It'll even take tree sap off your car's finish without scratching the paint! And use coconut or olive oil to polish furniture and wood floors, naturally.

Chocolate Chip Cheezecake Swirl

One bite of this dairy-free delight, and you'll be hooked on healthy, cruelty-free dessert. It's a kreamy white tart cheezecake with swirls of decadent chocolate sauce and the hidden crunch of real chocolate cacao nibs.

CRUST
- 1 cup almond meal
- ½ cup pitted Medjool or other semi-soft dates
- ¼ teaspoon sea salt

FILLING
- 3 cups cashews
- ¾ cup lemon juice
- ½ cup liquid coconut oil
- ½ cup agave syrup
- 2 recipes **Chocolate Sauce** (page 178)
- ¼ cup cacao nibs

To make the crust, combine the almond meal, dates, and salt in a mixing bowl and mix well. Press into the bottom of a springform cheesecake pan.

To make the filling, combine the cashews, lemon juice, coconut oil, and agave syrup in the high-speed blender and blend until smooth. Scoop half into the springform pan and top with half of the chocolate sauce. Use a knife to swirl the chocolate into the white batter. Sprinkle on the cacao nibs as a middle layer. Scoop the remaining cheesecake batter on top and swirl with the remaining chocolate sauce. Place in the freezer until firm, a few hours.

Will keep for several weeks in the freezer. Thaw for 20 minutes to soften before serving.

Tiramisu

MAKES 4 TO 6 SERVINGS

In this light layered cake, a "zabaglione" of blended bananas and cashews is sprinkled with nuts and my version of ground coffee and then dusted with cinnamon and chocolate powder. You'll be amazed at how much ground cacao nibs taste like ground coffee.

BASE
¼ cup cashews
¾ cup pecans

GROUND "COFFEE"
1 tablespoon cashews
3 tablespoons cacao nibs

"ZABAGLIONE" FILLING
1 cup ground cashews
6 ripe bananas
⅓ cup agave syrup
⅓ cup liquid coconut oil
1 tablespoon alcohol-free vanilla extract, or the seeds from 1 vanilla bean

TOPPING
2 tablespoons ground cinnamon
2 tablespoons cacao powder

To make the base, place the cashews in the food processor and process into tiny pieces. Add the pecans and pulse into small pieces. Be careful not to overprocess into a butter, but you do want a fine powder.

To make the ground "coffee," grind the cashews into a powder in the grinder. Transfer to a bowl. Grind the cacao nibs. Transfer to the bowl with ground cashews and mix together.

To make the filling, combine the cashews, bananas, agave syrup, coconut oil, and vanilla in the food processor and process until smooth.

To make the topping, mix the cinnamon and cacao powder in a bowl.

To assemble, sprinkle the base onto the bottom of the pan and spoon the filling on top. Then sprinkle with the "coffee" grounds and finish off with a dusting of topping. Using a sieve will make your final dusting easier.

Place in the freezer for an hour or two to firm up before serving.

Will keep in your refrigerator for a few days and in your freezer for several weeks. Thaw 10 to 15 minutes before serving.

Acai Cheezecake

Packed with antioxidants, beautiful, dark, purple acai is blended with sweet rich cashews and tart lemon juice for a delicious cheezecake filling. A crumbled pecan crust and a layer of banana slices complete the cake. So creamy and refreshing, you'll never go back to dairy-based cheesecake.

CRUST

1½ cups pecans
½ teaspoon sea salt
½ cup pitted Medjool or other semi-soft dates
2 tablespoons shredded coconut

FILLING

3 cups cashews
¾ cup lemon juice
½ cup liquid coconut oil
½ cup agave syrup
1 package (100 grams) frozen acai smoothie packs, thawed until liquid
1 banana, sliced

To make the crust, combine the pecans and salt in the food processor and gently pulse to mix. Add the dates and pulse to break the pecans into small pieces. Avoid overprocessing into a powder or butter.

Sprinkle the coconut onto the bottom of a springform cheesecake pan. Add the pecan mixture and press evenly to form a crust.

To make the filling, combine the cashews, lemon juice, coconut oil, agave syrup, and acai in the high-speed blender and blend until smooth. Add small splashes of water if the mixture is too thick and needs help moving in the blender.

Scoop half of the filling onto the crust. Arrange the sliced banana on top. Top with the rest of the filling. Place in the freezer until firm, a few hours.

Will keep for several weeks in the freezer. Thaw for 20 minutes to soften before serving. It's always best to eat the acai soon after it's defrosted for maximum nutritional bang.

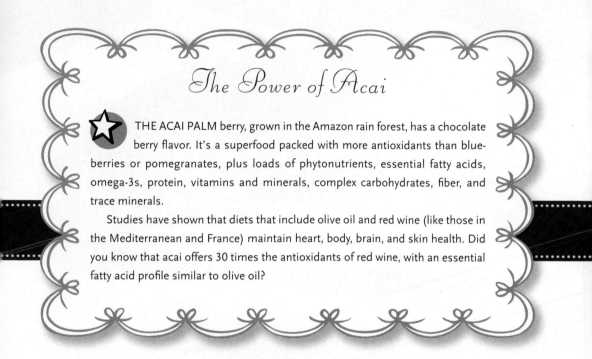

The Power of Acai

THE ACAI PALM berry, grown in the Amazon rain forest, has a chocolate berry flavor. It's a superfood packed with more antioxidants than blueberries or pomegranates, plus loads of phytonutrients, essential fatty acids, omega-3s, protein, vitamins and minerals, complex carbohydrates, fiber, and trace minerals.

Studies have shown that diets that include olive oil and red wine (like those in the Mediterranean and France) maintain heart, body, brain, and skin health. Did you know that acai offers 30 times the antioxidants of red wine, with an essential fatty acid profile similar to olive oil?

Strawberry Kream Cheezecake

MAKES 4 TO 6 SERVINGS

A kreamy cheeze filling is set on a thin almond flour crust and topped with a sweet strawberry sauce. Refrigeration will give this pie the texture of cream cheese. Use fresh strawberries if available, otherwise, use whole frozen ones, and defrost before using.

Note: This recipe uses lecithin powder as a thickener. Lecithin is an essential nutrient required by our bodies that's been found to increase brain power, strengthen the heart and liver, and dissolve fat and cholesterol. Lecithin powder comes from soy, so make sure to find one that's not genetically modified (non-GMO). If you'd like to leave lecithin out, increase the coconut oil to 1/4 cup and decrease the water to 1/3 cup.

CRUST

- 1 cup almond meal
- ¼ teaspoon sea salt
- ½ cup pitted Medjool or other semi-soft dates

FILLING

- 1 tablespoon grated lemon zest
- ½ cup lemon juice
- 1½ cups cashews
- ¾ cup filtered water
- 3 tablespoons liquid coconut oil
- Seeds from 2 vanilla beans or 2 tablespoons alcohol-free vanilla extract
- ¼ cup lecithin powder

TOPPING

- 1½ cups strawberries
- ⅓ cup agave syrup

To make the crust, combine the almond meal and salt in a mixing bowl. Sprinkle a pie pan lightly with some of this almond meal. Add the dates to the remaining almond meal and mix into a dough with your hands. Press the dough into the bottom of the pie pan as thinly as possible. The crust should reach at least halfway up the side of pan.

To make the filling, combine the zest, lemon juice, cashews, water, coconut oil, and vanilla in the high-speed blender and blend until smooth. Add the lecithin and blend to mix well and thicken. Scoop onto the crust. Refrigerate for 1 to 2 hours to firm up the filling.

To make the topping, combine the strawberries and agave syrup in the blender and pulse only a couple times to coarsely mix into a chunky sauce.

To serve, remove the cheezecake from the fridge, pour the sauce over the filling, and enjoy immediately.

The assembled cheesecake will keep for 2 to 3 days in the fridge. The filling and crust without the sauce will keep for up to 5 days in the fridge and several weeks in the freezer. The strawberry sauce will keep in the fridge a couple days when stored separately.

VARIATION:

Try substituting another sauce from the Sauces and Kreams chapter (page 165) for the strawberries and syrup. Pineapple sauce is delicious.

ANI'S RAW FOOD DESSERTS

Mini Chocolate Lava Cakes

MAKES 6 MINI CAKES

This is my version of flourless chocolate mini cakes with gooey chocolate lava oozing from the center and red raspberry sauce as a great complement to the rich chocolate cake. The upside-down cupcakes are molded in 1/2-cup tartlet cups and make beautiful personal cakes perfect for dinner with a special someone, or for larger dinner parties with friends.

3 cups dry walnuts
1 cup pitted Medjool dates
²⁄₃ cup cacao or carob powder
¼ teaspoon sea salt
Chocolate Sauce (page 178)
Raspberry Sauce (page 177)

To make the cake, combine the walnuts, dates, cacao powder, and salt in the food processor and process to mix well. Press about ½ cup each into 6 small ½-cup tartlet pans lined with plastic wrap, leaving deep tablespoon-sized cavities in the centers.

To serve, scoop 1 tablespoon of the chocolate sauce into the center of each tartlet cake. Flip upside down onto dessert plates, and release from pans. Remove the plastic wrap. Drizzle 1 to 2 tablespoons raspberry sauce over each and enjoy.

The cake and chocolate sauce will keep for at least 5 days in the fridge stored together or separately. The raspberry sauce will keep for 3 days in the fridge stored separately.

The Beauty of Figs

THEY TASTE DELICIOUS, look beautiful, have small seeds for great crunch, and add whole food sweetness. Figs—full of calcium, iron, magnesium, vitamin B_6, and potassium—are low in fat and high in fiber. They're a beauty food, plus a brain food. Here's what figs can do for us.

WEIGHT LOSS: Three fresh or dried figs have 5 grams of fiber. This soluble fiber slows the absorption of nutrients, keeps us feeling more satisfied after a meal, and helps cut down on snacking.

CLEAR SKIN: Fresh figs give skin the water it needs to stay clear and combat acne and oil. It also improves our skin's healthy glow.

BEAUTY SLEEP: Figs contain tryptophan for a good night's sleep.

BRAIN FUEL: The natural sugar in figs stimulates our brain to think quickly and help us recall information faster. It also helps our brain use glucose properly, and stimulates good circulation and beautiful skin and hair.

Fig Tartlets with Frangipane Kream

MAKES 4 TARTLETS

The filling for these country-style tartlets is sweet figs sun-kissed with orange, cinnamon, and vanilla and served on a walnut crust. Figs are a rich source of calcium, iron, magnesium, vitamin B6, and potassium. Low in fat and high in fiber, both fresh and dried figs are high in pectin, a soluble fiber that can reduce blood cholesterol.

CRUST
⅔ cups dry walnuts
Pinch salt
2 teaspoons agave syrup

FILLING
1½ cup dried figs, hard stems removed
1 tablespoon orange zest
1 tablespoon alcohol-free vanilla extract
½ teaspoon ground cinnamon

TOPPING
½ recipe **Almond Frangipane Kream**
(page 169)

To the make crust, combine the walnuts and salt in the food processor and pulse into small pieces. Be careful not to over-process; you don't want walnut butter. Add the agave syrup and pulse to mix. Line 4 small tartlet or brioche cups with plastic wrap. Use your fingertips to firmly press 2 tablespoons of crust into each.

To make the filling, combine the figs, zest, vanilla, and cinnamon in the food processor and process into small pieces. Use a scooper to top each tartlet crust with about 3 tablespoons filling.

To serve, top each tartlet with a dollop of kream.

Will keep for a couple weeks in the fridge.

Mango Sorbet–Macaroon Tartlets

MAKES 4 TARTLETS

Delicate coconut and cashew tartlet shells are filled with sweet, smooth mango sorbet. Mango contains high levels of beta-carotene, vitamins A and B$_2$, calcium, phosphorus, and iron for maintaining skin health. As early as 6,000 years ago, Native Americans treated mangoes as a noble item for enhancing beauty. Today, they are still called the fruit of love.

2 cups shredded coconut
½ cup cashews
¼ teaspoon salt
¼ cup agave syrup
Mango Sorbet (page 31)

To make the crust, combine the coconut, cashews, and salt in the food processor and process to fine powder. Add the agave syrup and process to mix well.

To make the tartlet shells, line 4 small tartlet or brioche cups with plastic wrap. Scoop about 2 tablespoons of the crust into each. Using your fingertips, firmly press the crust into the tartlet cup, leaving a cavity in the center to hold the sorbet. Place in the freezer to firm up for at least 30 minutes or more.

To serve, scoop 1 tablespoon mango sorbet into each tartlet shell and serve immediately.

The tartlet shells will keep in the freezer for many weeks. The assembled tartlets are best enjoyed immediately, but will keep in the freezer for several weeks. Thaw for 5 to 10 minutes before eating.

Lemon Pudding Filled Coconut Cupcakes

with Shaved Coconut Topping

MAKES 6 CUPCAKES

My biggest challenge to date has been making cupcakes for a six-year-old's birthday party. This recipe, the result of many trials and taste tests, was a huge hit with the kids, who are always our toughest fans. Packed with coconut for electrolytes, lemon juice for vitamin C, and bananas for potassium, these little gems keep us feeling great.

LEMON PUDDING
- ⅓ cup cashews
- 1½ bananas
- ¼ cup lemon juice (from 1 to 2 lemons)
- 2 tablespoons agave syrup

CUPCAKES
- 2½ cups dry pecans
- ½ cup shredded coconut
- ⅛ teaspoon sea salt
- ¾ cup firmly packed pitted Medjool dates
- 3 tablespoons alcohol-free vanilla extract

TOPPING
- ½ cup shaved or shredded coconut

To make the pudding, place the cashews in the Personal Blender with the grinder lid and 2-cup container or a food processor and grind into a powder. Add the bananas, lemon juice, and agave syrup and process until smooth. Place in the fridge to chill.

To make the cupcakes, combine the pecans, coconut, and salt in the food processor and process into evenly sized small pieces, taking care not to over-process into a butter. Scoop the mixture into another bowl. Combine the dates and vanilla in the food processor and process into small pieces. Return the pecan mixture to the food processor and pulse to mix. The cake mix should have a crumbly but sticky texture.

Place 6 cupcake liners in a muffin pan. Use a ½-cup measuring cup to scoop ½ cup loosely packed pecan mixture into each. Using your fingertips, gently press to firm up the cupcakes and create cavities in the centers to hold the pudding. Make sure the edges reach the tops of the cupcake liners.

To assemble, scoop about 3 tablespoons pudding into each cupcake and top with coconut. Place the muffin pan in the refrigerator to chill for several hours to firm up the cupcakes before serving.

The pudding will keep for a few days in fridge when stored separately. The cupcakes, stored separately, will keep for several weeks in the fridge. The assembled cupcakes will keep in the fridge for a few days.

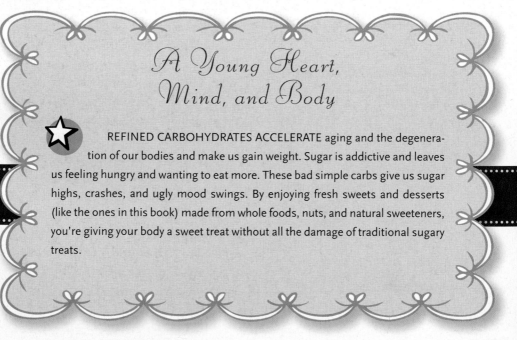

A Young Heart, Mind, and Body

REFINED CARBOHYDRATES ACCELERATE aging and the degeneration of our bodies and make us gain weight. Sugar is addictive and leaves us feeling hungry and wanting to eat more. These bad simple carbs give us sugar highs, crashes, and ugly mood swings. By enjoying fresh sweets and desserts (like the ones in this book) made from whole foods, nuts, and natural sweeteners, you're giving your body a sweet treat without all the damage of traditional sugary treats.

Carrot Cake Cupcakes with Kream Cheeze Frosting

MAKES 6 CUPCAKES

Everyone loves carrot cake. It's full of beta-carotene, which is good for our eyes of course, but it's also great for protecting our skin from sun damage. These carrot cakes are sweetened with dates, which hold together the almonds and carrot pulp. You'll need to make carrot juice to make the pulp needed in this recipe, or just visit your local juice bar.

CUPCAKES

2½ cups carrot pulp (from juicing about 1½ pounds carrots; see "Carrot Pulp and Applesauce," page 148)
1 cup almond meal powder
1½ teaspoons ground cinnamon
1 cup pitted Medjool dates
1⅓ cups shredded coconut

FROSTING

1½ cups cashews
2 tablespoons lemon juice (from about 1 lemon)
2 tablespoons agave syrup
½ cup filtered water, as needed

To make the cupcakes, combine the carrot pulp, almond meal, and cinnamon in a mixing bowl and mix well with a spoon or your hands. Add the dates and mix well. Add the coconut and mix well.

Place 6 cupcake liners in a muffin pan. Firmly press about ½ cup of the batter into each of the liners.

To make the frosting, combine the cashews, lemon juice, agave syrup, and ⅓ cup water in the high-speed blender and blend until smooth, adding additional water if needed.

To serve, frost each cupcake and enjoy.

The frosted cupcakes will keep for 4 or 5 days in the fridge.

Chocolate Crunch Cupcakes with Molten Mint Frosting

These beautiful chocolate cupcakes have crunch from cacao nibs and are topped with a sweet mint frosting. They're full of walnuts for vitamin E and dates for potassium, iron, and fiber. It all prevents sugar spikes, crashes, and mood swings, keeping us happy and feeling sexy.

FROSTING

- ¾ cup cashews
- ½ cup liquid coconut oil
- 1½ tablespoons firmly packed mint leaves, or 1 tablespoon dried mint, or 2½ teaspoons mint extract
- 3 tablespoons agave syrup
- 2 tablespoons filtered water
- ¼ teaspoon spirulina (optional), for color

CUPCAKES

- 2¼ cups dry walnuts
- ⅓ cup cacao or carob powder
- ¼ teaspoon sea salt
- ⅓ cup cacao nibs
- 1 cup pitted Medjool dates

To make the frosting, place the cashews in the Personal Blender with the grinder lid and 2-cup container or the food processor and grind into a fine powder. Scoop into a bowl. Combine the coconut oil and mint in the blender and blend until smooth, about 30 seconds. Add the cashew powder, agave syrup, water, and spirulina (if using) and blend until smooth. Place the frosting in the freezer to chill and thicken.

To make the cupcakes, combine the walnuts, cacao powder, and salt in the food processor and process into small uniform bits. Make sure to avoid over-processing into a butter. Add the cacao nibs and pulse to mix. Scoop into a bowl. Add the dates to the food processor and process into small pieces. Return the walnut mixture to the processor and pulse to mix. The mixture should have a crumbly, sticky texture.

Place 6 cupcake liners in a muffin pan. Use a ⅓-cup measuring cup or scooper to scoop about ⅓ cup of the crumble into each liner. Use your fingertips to gently press the crumble mixture into each cup to bind into a solid piece. Place the muffin pan in the fridge or freezer and chill for 1 hour, or until the cakes are firm.

To serve, test by removing a cupcake from the pan: If it's solid and doesn't crumble apart, it's ready to be frosted. The colder the frosting, the firmer it will be. Frost each cupcake and enjoy immediately.

Frosted cupcakes will keep for a week in the fridge. Unfrosted cupcakes will keep for several weeks in the fridge or freezer, and the frosting alone will keep for a week in fridge.

FROSTING SUGGESTION:
Scoop chilled frosting into a cake decorating bag with a decorative tip and have fun decorating the cupcakes.

Pack Your Snacks and Lunch

WANT TO SAVE lots of money? Take snacks and lunch to work each day. It's far more healthier for you, plus you'll use less packaging than the to-go containers and wraps from the sandwich shop.

All of these recipes make for delicious treats and meals. So take them with you to your workplace and pamper yourself!

3

Chocolate
and
Fudge

*A*LL CHOCOLATE COMES from a huge berry called the cacao pod, the fruit of the cacao tree. A pod contains 30 to 40 seeds or beans and each bean is made up of small cacao nibs. Cacao powder is ground nibs with the fat removed, and is usually raw. Cocoa powder, on the other hand, is "Dutch processed" using alkaline salts to help it dissolve more easily in liquid, and has lowered antioxidant values.

Real cacao chocolate is a superfood that is full of powerful antioxidants that help neutralize free radicals and the effects of aging. Cacao also supplies us with micronutrients like potassium, zinc, magnesium, and iron for radiant skin, healthy hair, and strong nails.

A study published by the *Journal of the American Medical Association* in 2003 found cacao lowers blood pressure, helping relax blood vessels so blood can flow through them easier. Luckily for your waistline, you only need a quarter of an ounce a day to reap the benefits; that is about one-seventh of a traditional chocolate bar. The caffeine in chocolate quickly increases alertness, and the tryptophan gives us a sensation of elation and ecstasy.

The flavonoids in cacao have been demonstrated in laboratory studies to have a greater antioxidant effect than blueberries, red wine, and green tea. A 1.5-ounce serving of cacao has as much antioxidant power as a glass of red wine.

The only downfall is that all chocolate contains caffeine, which triggers a stress response and a surge of adrenal hormones. So, moderation is key. Maca, a root from the Andes, is known as an adaptagen because it increases our ability to handle stress by strengthening our adrenal glands. I like to add a teaspoon or more of maca when using cacao to help offset the stress to my adrenals.

When a craving for chocolate kicks in, reach for these sweets filled only with superfoods that make you more powerful. They are simple to make: The base is made by mixing raw whole chocolate powder (cacao powder) into coconut oil, which hardens when chilled. Chocolates will keep for many weeks in the fridge or freezer.

Liquid Chocolate

Here is a **wonderful chocolate to be used as a topping for ice kreams or a dip for cookies, bananas, and strawberries. It is made by mixing together coconut oil and cacao powder. It's that simple.**

1 cup liquid coconut oil
½ cup cacao powder
1 tablespoon mesquite powder (optional)
1 tablespoon agave syrup (optional)

Place the coconut oil in a mixing bowl and whisk in the cacao powder, mesquite powder, and agave syrup (if using) until smooth. Use this liquid to dip or top your favorite chilled fruits and frozen treats.

Will keep for many weeks and months in your fridge. Can also be left at room temperature for several weeks.

VARIATIONS:

Try experimenting by flavoring the chocolate with fresh minced peppermint or peppermint extract, or vanilla beans or vanilla extract.

Cacao Butter

TO MAKE A chocolate that can withstand the sun and heat the same way a cooked chocolate bar can, use cacao butter instead of coconut oil. Cacao butter is the solid that's left after cacao powder is made, and melts at a higher temperature than coconut oil. If cacao butter is available in your area, here's how to liquefy it: Thinly shave the cacao butter. Place in a bowl, then place that bowl into another larger bowl filled with hot water. Use the liquid cacao butter in place of the liquid coconut oil, and then chill to set. After that, you can keep it at room temperature.

Chocolate Raisin Bark

Chocolate Raisin Bark is a guiltless, good-for-you superfood treat that literally takes a minute to make (plus chilling time). Packed full of antioxidants, this is real chocolate, made from the cacao straight off the tree without any added fillers or waxes. The coconut oil and caffeine will increase your metabolism and help you burn more calories and fat.

½ cup raisins and/or nuts
Liquid Chocolate (page 74)

Stir the raisins and/or nuts into the liquid chocolate. Spread on a sheet tray lined with waxed paper and put in the fridge or freezer for 5 to 10 minutes to solidify. Break into pieces and enjoy.

Will keep for many weeks or months in the fridge. Can also be left at room temperature for several weeks.

Chocolate-Covered Bananas

MAKES 4 SERVINGS

$\mathcal{W}hat\ could\ be$ better than frozen bananas dipped in real chocolate and sprinkled with your favorite toppings? Since I'm never able to eat an entire frozen banana myself, my recipe calls for using bananas cut in half. Feel free to make 4 full-sized bananas if that suits your fancy.

If you need to liquefy or thin the consistency of the liquid chocolate, place it in a bowl and place that bowl in a bowl of hot water. The warmer the chocolate, the thinner the chocolate coating will be. If the liquid chocolate is too thin, cool it by placing its bowl in a larger bowl of ice while stirring. Remove when desired consistency.

4 bananas, peeled and halved crosswise to make 8 shorter pieces
Favorite toppings such as chopped nuts, coconut, hemp nuts
Liquid Chocolate (page 74)

Skewer the banana halves on 8 wooden skewers and place in the freezer for several hours until frozen.

Place the toppings in flat dishes. Scoop the liquid chocolate into a cup for easy dipping. Dip each banana skewer into the chocolate, then roll the coated banana in a topping to stick.

Transfer the coated bananas to a sheet tray lined with parchment paper and place in the freezer until the chocolate hardens, just a couple minutes.

Will keep for a several weeks or more in the freezer.

Chocolate-Dipped Strawberries

MAKES 4 TO 6 SERVINGS

Beautiful strawberries dipped in real deal chocolate are a nutritional powerhouse. Antioxidant-rich strawberries are great for our skin, while cacao increases circulation.

The warmer the chocolate, the thinner it will be and the thinner the coating will be. If too thin, you can either dip a strawberry again once the first coat has hardened or you can cool the dipping chocolate a bit by placing the bowl in another bowl of ice and continuing to stir until desired thickness. Then, remove bowl from ice, and dip, dip, dip!

12-long stemmed strawberries
½ recipe **Liquid Chocolate** (page 74)

Chill cleaned strawberries in the fridge for at least 30 minutes. Remove from the fridge and dip in the chocolate, placing the dipped strawberry on a sheet tray lined with parchment paper. Place in the fridge to set.

Will last a few days refrigerated, depending on freshness of the strawberries.

Filled Chocolate Truffles

MAKES ABOUT 12 TRUFFLES

$\mathcal{Y}ou'll\ need\ to$ **use a metal chocolate mold tray for this recipe (see photo on page 15). Chill the tray in the freezer first, so when you pour in the chocolate it solidifies immediately. Then fill with your favorite jam, sauce, or kream and seal it closed with a final chocolate pour.**

1 tablespoon olive oil
½ recipe **Liquid Chocolate** (page 74)
¼ cup favorite filling such as jam,
    sauce, kream, berries

Evenly oil 12 mold cavities with olive oil and place in the freezer to chill for at least 30 minutes. To test that it's cold enough, drop a small amount of liquid chocolate onto it; it should solidify right away.

Place a sheet of parchment paper on the counter. Pour the liquid chocolate carefully into the chilled tray cavities. Avoid spilling outside the molds. Let set a few seconds, and then turn upside down to empty the liquid chocolate left in molds onto the parchment. Turn right side up. The molds should be lined with a thin layer of solid chocolate. Use a butter knife or spoon to clean the edges around the outside of each mold.

Place jam, sauce, or kream into the cavity of each chocolate mold. Pour on another layer of liquid chocolate to fill each mold to the brim and seal them closed. Place the filled tray in the freezer to harden for several minutes.

Remove the mold from the freezer and turn upside down over parchment paper or a tray and tap to release the filled chocolates from the tray. Enjoy immediately, or keep chilled in fridge.

Will keep for several days in fridge, depending on the shelf life of the filling.

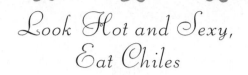

Look Hot and Sexy, Eat Chiles

THE CAPSAICIN IN spicy chile peppers counteracts inflammation and premature aging of the skin and is a fat burner and appetite suppressant. Capsaicin is the active ingredient in many of the most popular "fat burning" supplements on the market. It increases our metabolic activity, helping us burn calories and fat. Plus, it increases blood flow to keep our skin looking nourished, oxygenated, and vital.

Mayan Crunch Truffle Balls

MAKES ABOUT 10 SERVINGS

Hot chili and cinnamon spice up moist truffles made with ground cashews and cacao nibs. The treats are great for powering your long hike, run, or cycling trip. They travel well and don't need refrigeration.

1 cup dry cashews
½ teaspoon ground cinnamon
⅛ to ¼ teaspoon chili powder, to taste
⅛ teaspoon sea salt
¾ cup cacao nibs
⅓ cup agave syrup
Cacao powder or additional ground cinnamon, for rolling

Grind small batches of the cashews into a fine powder using a coffee grinder. (I grind ½ cup at a time using the Personal Blender with the grinder lid on the 1-cup container.) Scoop into a mixing bowl and add the cinnamon, chili powder, and salt and mix well.

Grind the cacao nibs into a fine powder. Add to the cashew mixture and mix well. Add the agave syrup and mix well. Use a 1½-tablespoon scooper to drop dough onto a plate, or your hands to roll into balls.

To serve, roll the balls in 2 to 3 tablespoons of cacao powder or ground cinnamon. Enjoy immediately or place in the fridge or freezer for 30 minutes or more if you'd like them firmer.

Will keep for a couple weeks or more at room temperature. Will keep a month or more in the fridge.

Lavender Chocolate Bars

MAKES 12 SERVINGS

This delicate, floral-scented chocolate showcases lavender. To harvest fresh lavender, select the freshest-looking flowers with the fullest color. Immerse all the blooms in water a few times to remove insects and soil. Then lay the flowers on towels and pat dry or gently spin dry in a salad spinner.

1 cup liquid coconut oil
3 tablespoons agave syrup
¼ cup fresh lavender flowers or 1½ tablespoons dried
¾ cup cacao powder
¼ cup almond butter
1 cup almonds, coarsely chopped by pulsing in food processor
1 cup raisins
⅓ cup sliced almonds

In the high-speed blender, combine the coconut oil, agave syrup, and lavender flowers. Process for 30 to 60 seconds, checking that the mixture is not getting too hot, until smooth. Add the cacao and almond butter and blend slowly on low speed until well mixed.

Transfer to a mixing bowl, add the chopped almonds and raisins, and mix well.

Spread the mixture onto a sheet tray lined with parchment paper in a ½ to 1-inch layer. Top with the sliced almonds. Place in the freezer to chill until solid, about 15 minutes. Break into pieces and serve.

Will keep for a month or more in the freezer.

Chocolate–Cashew Butter Fudge

MAKES 8 SERVINGS

This smooth, rich fudge, best enjoyed chilled, is sweetened with low-glycemic mesquite powder, a nutritious powder ground from mesquite pods. The healthy treat is high in protein and rich in lysine, calcium, iron, zinc, and potassium to help rebuild the collagen in our skin.

1 cup cashew butter
¼ cup cacao powder
2 tablespoons mesquite powder
2 tablespoons agave syrup
2 tablespoons liquid coconut oil
1 tablespoon cacao nibs

Combine the cashew butter, cacao powder, mesquite powder, agave syrup, and coconut oil in a large bowl and mix well. Use a 1½-tablespoon scooper to scoop balls onto a sheet tray lined with parchment paper. Top each with a few pieces of cacao nibs. Enjoy immediately, or place in the refrigerator for an hour to firm up. Best stored and served from the refrigerator.

Will keep for a month or more in the fridge.

4

Crisps
and
Cobblers

*T*HESE EASY-TO-MAKE crisps and cobblers are combinations of sweet, juicy, fresh fruits and crunchy, nutritious nuts. The base of my crusts are made with about half crushed nuts bound together with sticky dried fruit like figs or dates. The filling is sliced fruit tossed in a bit of agave syrup for sweetness, plus spices for exciting flavor.

Antioxidant-rich blueberries and almonds make up the Spiced Blueberry Cobbler, sweet pears and figs with almonds create the Pear Ginger Crisp, and beautiful nectarines and raspberries with rich, maple-flavored pecans make a scrumptious Nectarine-Raspberry Crumble that's good for our health and good for our planet.

Fresh fruits are mostly water and hydrate our bodies while cleansing and detoxifying. High in enzymes, fruits are easy to digest and packed full of cancer-fighting, age-defying vitamins, minerals, essential fatty acids, and antioxidants.

My cobblers will keep a few days in your fridge, but are usually gobbled up right away.

Pear Ginger Crisp

With pears for sweet juiciness and almonds and figs for crunch, this crisp is delicious for both breakfast and as the end to any meal—and a delicious low-calorie way to up your antioxidant intake. Enjoying pears with their skin will give you more fiber, in addition to potassium, copper, and vitamin C.

CRUST
¾ cup dried figs
1 cup dry almonds
¾ teaspoon salt

FILLING
4 cups sliced pitted pears (3 or 4 pears)
1 tablespoon minced fresh ginger
1 teaspoon ground cinnamon

To make the crust, place the figs in the food processor and process into small pieces. If you find the figs too sticky, you can also chop them by hand. Add the almonds and salt and process into medium-sized pieces (not too small, and big enough to keep the crunch of the almonds).

To make the filling, toss the pear slices with the ginger and cinnamon in a mixing bowl to mix well. Scoop into a loaf pan, top with the crust, and serve.

Will keep for 1 day in the fridge. The crust will keep for several weeks when stored separately in the fridge.

VARIATION:
Substitute half of the pears in the filling with 2 cups sliced fresh figs.

Nectarine-Raspberry Crumble

MAKES 4 TO 6 SERVINGS

Nectarines and raspberries are terrific "good carb" sources of vitamin C for keeping us beautiful on the inside and out. The antioxidants and phytonutrients giving them their gorgeous bright color will protect our skin from damaging UV rays. Mother Nature has perfectly planned to have these fruits available for us to enjoy fresh during the sunniest season of the year.

CRUST
- ½ cup pitted semi-soft dates
- ⅓ cup pecans
- ¼ teaspoon sea salt

FILLING
- 2 cups sliced nectarines (2 or 3 nectarines)
- 2 to 4 tablespoons agave syrup, to taste
- 2 cups raspberries (about 1 pint)

To make the crust, combine the dates, pecans, and salt in the food processor and process into small pieces. Make sure not to overprocess into butter; you want a crumble texture.

To make the filling, combine the nectarines and agave syrup in a mixing bowl and toss to mix well. Add the raspberries and gently mix. Scoop into a loaf pan, top with the crust, and serve.

Will keep for 1 to 2 days in the refrigerator. The crumble crust will keep for several weeks when stored on its own in fridge.

Spiced Blueberry Cobbler

The sweetness of blueberries with a hint of chai spices means big flavor in this easy cobbler. Blueberries have powerful antioxidants and are packed with vitamins A, B, and C to help prevent skin damage caused by stress and the sun. Fresh blueberries are one of the many fruits I enjoy picking in the summertime. They're delicious straight off the vine and in this crunchy cobbler.

CRUST
- 1 cup dry almonds
- 1 teaspoon ground nutmeg
- 1 teaspoon ground cinnamon
- ½ teaspoon salt
- 1 cup pitted semi-soft Medjool dates

FILLING
- 4 cups blueberries
- ¼ cup agave syrup (optional)

To make the crust, combine the almonds, nutmeg, cinnamon, and salt in the food processor and pulse into coarse pieces. Add the dates and process until mixed well. Sprinkle half of the crust into the bottom of a loaf pan.

To make the filling, combine the blueberries and agave syrup (if using) in a mixing bowl and toss to mix well. Scoop into the loaf pan. Top with the remaining crust, press gently, and serve.

Will keep for 2 to 3 days in the fridge. The crust will keep for several weeks when stored on its own in fridge.

SERVING SUGGESTION:
Serve the cobbler parfait-style in a glass: Start with about ½ cup of cobbler in the bottom of the a glass. Add a scoop of your favorite ice kream and top with another ¼ to ½ cup cobbler.

Peach and Pistachio Cobbler

MAKES 4 TO 6 SERVINGS

Peaches are rich in phytochemicals, vitamin C, and beta-carotene, promoting healthy, radiant skin, boosting our immune system, and helping us detoxify.

CRUST
- ½ cup shelled pistachios
- ¼ teaspoon sea salt
- ½ cup semi-soft pitted Medjool dates

FILLING
- 4 cups sliced pitted peaches (about 4 peaches)
- 3 tablespoons agave syrup
- 1 tablespoon alcohol-free vanilla extract, or the seeds from 1 vanilla bean

To make the crust, combine the pistachios and salt in the food processor and process into medium-size pieces. Add the dates and process to mix well.

To make the filling, combine the peaches, agave syrup, and vanilla in a mixing bowl and mix well. Scoop into a loaf pan, top with the crust, and serve.

Will keep in the fridge for 1 day. The crust will keep for several weeks when stored alone in the fridge.

Exercise Is Fun

EXERCISE KEEPS US fit and at our ideal weight, makes us powerful and strong, and keeps us looking sexy. It can be hard to keep hands off an active body with natural muscle tone that looks beautiful.

Exercise stimulates our lymphatic system and helps it clear toxins, waste, and infection from all tissues. It keeps us physically strong and helps relieve stress and tension. Our largest organ is our skin, and pumping our heart improves circulation, sending fresh nutrients and oxygen to feed all of our skin for a clear complexion that glows.

Instead of weight loss, focus on strength, fitness, and well-being. Increasing our muscle mass increases our metabolism. Muscle feeds on fat, and focusing on strength will burn away flab. Sitting in a sauna a couple times a week also helps us sweat out toxins while burning extra calories.

Food allergens cause allergic, inflammatory response in our bodies like swelling and bloating. To help your body shrink and be smaller all over and decrease inflammation and swelling, eliminate common food allergens like eggs, fish, corn products, and coffee. Avoid trans fats and saturated fats from dairy, meats, and refined oils and refined carbohydrates like sugar and white flour. Add more fiber and water to your diet to help you tighten up, shrink down, and even slow the signs of aging.

Country-Style Apple Oat Cobbler

MAKES 4 TO 6 SERVINGS

Fresh apples tossed with vanilla are served amongst a crumble of oats sweetened with dates and a hint of cinnamon. This cobbler is delicious with all different types of apples throughout the year. A real comfort food.

CRUST
- 1 cup raw oats
- 1 teaspoon ground cinnamon
- 1 cup pitted Medjool dates

FILLING
- 4 cups sliced cored apples (about 3 apples)
- ¼ cup agave syrup
- 1 tablespoon alcohol-free vanilla extract, or the seeds from 1 vanilla bean

To make the crust, combine the oats and cinnamon in the food processor and process into small pieces. Add the dates and process to mix well. Sprinkle half of the crust onto the bottom of a loaf pan.

To make the filling, combine the apples, agave syrup, and vanilla in a mixing bowl and toss to mix. Scoop over the crust in the loaf pan, top with remaining crust, and serve.

Will keep for 3 to 4 days in the fridge.

Apricot Lovers' Cobbler

MAKES 4 TO 6 SERVINGS

If you're not already crazy about apricots, this recipe will turn you into a bona fide apricot lover! The crumble crust is dried apricots and pistachios, and the filling is fresh apricots sliced and tossed in an aromatic vanilla-agave syrup.

CRUST
½ cup dried apricots
¼ teaspoon sea salt
½ cup shelled pistachios

FILLING
4 cups sliced pitted fresh apricots
(about 8 apricots)
¼ cup agave syrup
1 tablespoon alcohol-free vanilla extract,
or the seeds from 1 vanilla bean

To make the crust, combine the dried apricots and salt in the food processor and process into a paste. Add the pistachios and process to mix well. Sprinkle half of the crust onto the bottom of a loaf pan.

To make the filling, combine the fresh apricots, agave syrup, and vanilla in a mixing bowl and toss well. Scoop onto the crust in the loaf pan, top with remaining crust, and serve.

Will keep for 1 to 2 days in the fridge. When stored separately in the fridge, the crust will keep for a week or more and the filling will keep for a day or two.

5

Puddings and Parfaits

*T*HE MOST DELICIOUS and nutritious mylks and kreams can easily be made in your blender from nuts and seeds. Nuts and seeds are miracle foods. They are packed with nutrients like protein that feed our skin and collagen; and vitamin E to reverse aging and prevent oxidation damage to cells and skin; vitamin B for healthy eyes, skin, nails, and hair; and zinc to fight acne and help our skin heal and rebuild.

Who knew trifles, fondue, and melba could be vegan and raw? It's as easy as blending up nuts or avocado with a fruit sweetener and spices to make dreamy, rich, smooth kreams.

The mylks, kreams, and ice kreams in my book are all cholesterol-free, healthy, guilt-free, and cruelty-free. That's why I use alternate spellings, to show that they are different from dairy products.

Unlike dairy, they don't cause inflammation, which means you'll look and feel better. Give them a try, and you'll find yourself saying, "Holy cow, this is delicious!"

Mini Berry Trifles

MAKES 4 SERVINGS

Here's my modern, ultra-fresh version of a trifle, a beautiful layered dessert of red raspberry syrup and creamy rich almond kream topped with fresh berries.

Raspberry Sauce (page 177)
Almond Frangipane Kream (page 169)
2 cups blackberries, blueberries, strawberries, and/or raspberries

Scoop the **Raspberry Sauce** into the bottoms of 4 mini trifle glasses. Carefully add a layer of almond kream. Gently top with the berries and serve.

Will keep in your refrigerator for 1 to 2 days.

Tropical Fruit Parfait

MAKES 4 SERVINGS

A parfait is a beautifully layered dessert of fruit, syrup, and cream. This one is gorgeous with orange and yellows from mango, pineapple, and banana. You can choose to use dark purple Acai Sauce to contrast, or a yellow pineapple sauce to match. It's that easy to make eating fresh fruit fun and delicious!

Acai Sauce (page 178) or **Pineapple Sauce** (page 175)
1½ cups sliced mango (about 1 large mango)
1½ cups sliced pineapple
1 banana, sliced
Coconut Kream (page 171)

Spoon the sauce into 4 parfait glasses. Top with layers of mango, pineapple, and banana, then top with the kream.

Will keep for a day in the refrigerator.

Peach Melba

Peach Melba is **a classic French dessert that combines poached peaches with raspberry sauce and vanilla ice cream. It's a lovely summer dessert when made with peak-season fruit. The three components here can be prepared ahead of time, so the assembly can be very quick just before serving. Peaches from the local farmers' market are full of sweet juicy flavor. Yellow peaches are beautiful, but the sweetness of white peaches is a nice complement, too.**

2 peaches, pitted and sliced
2 tablespoons agave syrup
Coconut Ice Kream (page 35)
Raspberry Sauce (page 177)

Place the sliced peaches in a mixing bowl and drizzle with the agave syrup. Set aside. The longer you leave the peaches, the more they'll soften and "poach."

Divide the sliced peaches among 4 serving glasses. Top with a scoop of ice kream and drizzle with **Raspberry Sauce.** Serve immediately.

Hemp-Goji Acai Bowl

MAKES 4 SERVINGS

Acai, a dark purple palm berry from the Amazon in Brazil, is nature's energy and beauty fruit. Its taste reminds me of dark berries or red wine and chocolate. With twice the amount of antioxidants as pomegranates, along with vitamins C and E and EFAs, acai combats aging and keeps cell membranes and skin supple. It contains more calcium than dairy milk.

ACAI

- 3 packages (100 grams each) frozen acai smoothie packs
- 1 banana
- ¾ cup pecans
- ⅓ to ½ cup filtered water, as needed
- ¼ cup agave syrup (optional)

TOPPINGS

- 4 tablespoons hemp nuts
- 4 tablespoons goji berries

Place the acai, banana, pecans, water, and agave syrup (if using) in the high-speed blender and blend until smooth.

To serve, scoop the acai mixture into 4 glasses or bowls and top each with 1 tablespoon hemp nuts and 1 tablespoon goji berries. Serve immediately.

Carob Fondue

This is a deliciously decadent, creamy, and velvety smooth chocolate-like fondue. Carob is caffeine-free, plus it has a great malty flavor. You can make it with the same amount of cacao powder if you prefer the flavor and kick of chocolate.

Avocado gives this fondue its smooth, rich texture and complex flavor. Avocado is loaded with nutritional goodies that keep our complexion nourished and moist, like vitamin E and good-for-us monounsaturated fats.

⅓ cup pitted Medjool dates
¼ cup agave syrup
½ cup ripe avocado flesh (from 1 medium avocado)
½ to 1 cup filtered water, to desired consistency
⅓ cup carob powder

Combine the dates and agave syrup in the food processor and process until smooth. Add the avocado and process until smooth. Add ½ cup of the water and carob powder and process until mixed well, adding more water to reach desired consistency. You may need to scrape the sides of the food processor to mix everything well.

Serve with fruit like orange slices, berries, and bananas, and even **Breakfast Toast** (page 149).

6

Cookies

COOKIES ARE ALWAYS a great congratulatory, self-indulgent, sweet treat. They hold off hungry after-school kids until dinnertime, make for yummy lunchbox surprises, and are fun for birthdays and dinner parties. Homemade cookies always taste the best and are easy to make—especially when they don't need baking!

Raw cookie dough is made by mixing a sticky ingredient like dates, raisins, figs, or nut butter with a dry ingredient to bind it together. The result is a texture similar to that of an under-baked gooey cookie. Oatmeal Raisin Cookie dough is made with sweet dates and raisins mixed with ground dry oats and a hint of cinnamon. Almond Goji Cacao Chip Cookie dough is made with sticky almond butter mixed with dry almond meal, then tossed with superfoods like goji berries and cacao nibs. And, the Lemon Fig Cookie dough is made with sweet, crunchy figs mixed with dry cashews, sticky cashew butter, and kissed with tart lemon zest. It's all about the alchemy of flavors and textures.

Raw cookies are super easy, fast, and fun to make. Simply mix the dough, then press into cookie cutters to make fun shapes or roll into balls and flatten into cookies. Kids love using their hands to mix up the dough and shape the cookies: This is real play food.

Oatmeal Raisin Cookies

Here's a modern version of old-fashioned cookies with the sweet maple flavor of Medjool dates, a sprinkling of raisins, and a hint of cinnamon. The recipe calls for raw oats: If they are not available in your area, you'll find them at my online store at *www.AniPhyo.com*. Regular quick oats or steel cut oats will work, too, though they are not technically raw, as they're cooked during processing. Your cookies will still taste delicious either way.

1 cup raw oats
1 teaspoon ground cinnamon
½ cup firmly packed pitted Medjool dates
½ cup raisins

Combine the oats and cinnamon in the food processor and process into small pieces. Add the dates and process to mix well. Add the raisins and pulse to mix.

Press about 3 tablespoons of the dough into cookie cutters on a sheet tray lined with parchment, or roll the dough into balls and flatten.

Serve immediately or store in sealed container or bag.

Will keep for a week at room temperature or for many weeks in the refrigerator or freezer. Thaw for 15 minutes before eating.

Carob Walnut Cookies

MAKES 8 TO 12 COOKIES

Sweet raisins, malty **carob, and rich walnuts are ground together to make a delicious, dark, sweet cookie. Packed with antioxidants, vitamin E, and EFAs, these cookies keep you trim and your skin radiant.**

1 cup raisins
¾ cup raw walnuts
¼ cup raw carob powder
1 teaspoon mesquite powder (optional)
⅛ teaspoon sea salt

Combine the raisins, walnuts, carob powder, mesquite powder if using, and salt in the food processor. Process until the dough begins sticking together.

Press the dough into 2-inch cookie cutters placed on a sheet tray lined with parchment paper. Shoot for a thickness of ⅓- to ½-inch. Or, make 1- to 1½-inch balls and flatten.

Place the cookies in the freezer to chill and firm up for 30 minutes or more before serving or transferring to the fridge for serving later.

Will keep for many weeks in the fridge or freezer. Thaw 5 minutes before eating.

Almond-Goji Cacao Chip Cookies

MAKES 12 COOKIES

Whole cacao nibs **are married to the nutty rich flavor of smooth almond butter and almond meal in these easy superfood cookies. Hits of goji berries provide 19 different amino acids, more vitamin C than oranges, and a wide variety of antioxidants, vitamin E, vitamin B, and essential fatty acids. Cacao nibs, especially when cold, have a great crunch.**

½ cup almond butter
3 tablespoons agave syrup
2 tablespoons alcohol-free vanilla
    extract, or seeds from 2 vanilla beans
¼ teaspoon sea salt
1½ cups almond meal
¼ cup goji berries
3 tablespoons cacao nibs

Stir together the almond butter, agave syrup, vanilla, and salt in a mixing bowl. Add the almond meal, goji berries, and cacao nibs and mix well.

Drop the dough by 1½ tablespoons onto a sheet tray lined with parchment paper. Use a fork to press the balls into flattened cookies, as you would for peanut butter cookies. Serve right away, or freeze for an hour to firm up.

Will keep for many weeks in the fridge or freezer. Thaw 5 minutes before eating.

VARIATION:
If you're not in the mood for caffeine, try replacing the cacao nibs with the same amount of goji berries, or better yet, dried mulberries. I had my first fresh mulberries this summer, and they're my new favorite. If you can't find dried mulberries, look for them on my website, *www.AniPhyo.com.*

Halva Chia Thumbprint Cookies

MAKES 9 COOKIES

These fun cookies are inspired by a Balkan-style, calcium-rich, tahini-based halva. You can get sprouted chia seed powder from Navitas Naturals. Or, you can use dry chia seeds, unsoaked and ground into a powder in a grinder. Or, substitute ground flaxseed powder, which provides many similar nutritional benefits.

¾ cup sprouted chia seed powder
½ cup tahini
¾ cup almond meal
¼ teaspoon salt
¼ cup agave syrup
⅓ cup pitted semi-soft MedJool dates
2 tablespoons **Raspberry Sauce** (page 177) or **Persimmon Jam** (page 151)

Combine the chia seed powder, tahini, almond meal, and salt in a mixing bowl and mix well. Add the agave syrup and mix well. Add the dates and mix with your hands or a spoon.

Roll the dough into 9 balls (about 2 tablespoons each) and place on a sheet tray lined with parchment paper. Use your thumb or the end of a wooden spoon to make an indentation into the center of each cookie. Fill each with a generous ½ teaspoon sauce or jam.

To make the flower-shaped cookies in the photo, place the dough in the center of a flower-shaped cookie cutter on a sheet tray lined with parchment paper. Press to ⅓- to ½-inch thick, and then make an indentation in the center to fill with jam.

To serve, chill in the refrigerator for 20 minutes or more to firm up.

Will keep for several days in the fridge or many weeks when stored separately from jam.

Mulberry Pecan Cookies

MAKES 12 COOKIES

These gooey, sticky, chewy cookies are packed with sweet white mulberries and pecan pieces and sweetened with thick yacon syrup, a natural low-glycemic, low-calorie sweetener that tastes like caramel and molasses.

I recently discovered fresh and dried mulberries, a functional, nutrient-rich food full of antioxidants, vitamin C, iron, and protein. They're like blackberries with smaller seeds and come in white, red, and purple variations. Some are long, some are short; they are all sweet and delicious.

Dried white mulberries and yacon syrup are available from Navitas Naturals. See "Yacon Power" (page) for more information. And visit me online for more information at *www.AniPhyo.com*.

½ cup almond meal
¼ cup almond butter
¼ cup yacon syrup or agave syrup
1 cup dried mulberries
¼ cup pecans, crushed

Combine the almond meal, almond butter, and yacon syrup in a mixing bowl and mix well. Add the mulberries and pecans and mix well.

Scoop the dough by 1½ tablespoons onto a sheet tray lined with parchment and flatten with a fork.

Refrigerate for 30 minutes to firm up before serving.

Will keep for several weeks or more in the fridge.

VARIATION:

To up the chewy, gooey, stickiness, use another 1 to 2 tablespoons yacon syrup. You'll get cookies reminiscent of caramel turtles.

Pecan Pie Cookies

MAKES 10 COOKIES

Treat yourself to a holiday celebration every day with these delicious cookies. They are sweetened with dates, packed with pecans, and spiced with cinnamon and a hint of orange. They travel well, so keep them in your backpack or bag for a quick healthy snack.

1 cup pecans
1 teaspoon ground cinnamon
1 teaspoon orange oil or orange juice
1 cup pitted Medjool dates

Combine the pecans, cinnamon, and orange oil in the food processor and pulse into small chunks. Add the dates and process until mixed well.

Scoop the dough by 1½ tablespoons onto a sheet tray lined with parchment and flatten into cookies.

Will keep for a week in the fridge or several weeks in the freezer (thaw before eating).

Lemon Fig Cookies

MAKES 12 COOKIES

These sweet-tart cookies with the snap of fig are packed with antioxidants and vitamin C. Figs are also high in calcium—ideal for growing children and the development of strong bones.

½ cup dried figs, hard stems removed
½ cup dry cashews
1 tablespoon grated lemon zest (from 1 to 2 lemons)
¼ teaspoon sea salt
¼ cup cashew butter

Process the figs into small pieces in the food processor. Place in a bowl. Process the cashews, lemon zest, and salt into small pieces in the processor. Return the figs to the food processor with the cashews. Add the cashew butter and process to mix well.

Scoop the dough by 1½ tablespoons onto a sheet tray lined with parchment paper. Flatten to about ½-inch thick.

Serve immediately or chill in the refrigerator.

Will keep for at least a week in the fridge.

Exfoliate and Moisturize for Age-Defying Skin

OUR SKIN CELLS renew every three weeks or so, but this renewal process slows down as we age. By removing the uppermost layer of our epidermis, we help speed up the turning over of dead, dull skin, while stimulating the creation of new cells. When I'm eating right and getting enough EFAs, my skin stays moist and hydrated, but it always helps to exfoliate as well.

Fruit enzymes are great for exfoliating, especially when you have overripe fruit on hand. Mash up papaya, pineapple, or grapefruit—all high in vitamin C and age-defying antioxidants—and place on your clean face for 20 to 30 minutes, then rinse off. Goodbye dead skin cells, hello smooth, hydrated, glowing skin.

After exfoliating, I like to apply jojoba oil or coconut oil to my newer, fresher skin cells. Sometimes I'll use hemp oil, flax oil, or olive oil. I also put these in my hair for smooth, moisturizing shine.

Having beautiful skin doesn't need to cost a lot or take much time. Anti-aging skin care is easy. By eating-nutrient-rich foods, we beautify from the inside out. By exfoliating, we get rid of the dead dull old skin cells on the surface to let our inner glow shine through.

Cherry Brownie Hearts

MAKES 4 TO 6 BROWNIES

These delicious whole food brownies feature tart dried cherries sweetened with mesquite powder for protein, calcium, and minerals. A brownie can double as a meal, or a vitamin and mineral supplement, fueling your body and keeping you trim, lean, and beautiful.

½ cup dry almonds
¼ cup mesquite powder
3 tablespoons cacao beans
¼ teaspoon sea salt
2 tablespoons liquid coconut oil
1 tablespoon alcohol-free vanilla extract, or the seeds from 1 vanilla bean
1 cup nonsulphured dried cherries
⅓ cup pitted semi-soft dates

Combine the almonds, mesquite powder, cacao beans, and salt in the food processor and process into small pieces. Add the coconut oil and vanilla and process to mix well. Add the cherries and dates and mix well.

Place a heart-shaped cookie cutter on a sheet tray lined with parchment paper. Press about 2 tablespoons of the dough into the center to form a brownie. Repeat with the remaining dough. Or line a loaf pan with parchment paper, add the dough, and press evenly. Chill in the freezer for at least 30 minutes to firm up before serving.

Will keep for several weeks in the fridge or freezer.

VARIATION:

Heart-shaped cherry brownies are pictured here dipped in **Liquid Chocolate** (page 74) and garnished with **Candied Citrus Zest** (page 157).

Sesame Snap Cookies

Sweet apricots confettied with pistachio and sesame seeds create a beautiful sweet-tart cookie that's easy to make and can be enjoyed immediately with your favorite smoothie.

1 cup dried apricots
½ cup shelled pistachios
½ cup sesame seeds
1 teaspoon lemon extract or lemon juice
1 teaspoon agave syrup

Place the apricots in the food processor and process into a paste. Add the pistachios, sesame seeds, lemon extract, and agave syrup and process to mix well.

Scoop the dough by 1½ tablespoons onto a sheet tray lined with parchment and flatten into cookies.

Will keep for a week in the fridge or for several weeks in the freezer (thaw before eating).

VARIATIONS:

If you love herbs, try adding ½ teaspoon fresh thyme or tarragon to the dough. Or add ½ teaspoon minced fresh ginger for zing.

Trail Mix Cookies

What a great idea: trail mix inside a delicious cookie! Crunchy almonds, rich walnuts, and sunflower seeds are sweetened with dates and raisins and a hint of cinnamon. These cookies travel well, so take them on your next hike, and see for yourself how yummy they are when enjoyed in nature.

¾ cup almonds
1 teaspoon ground cinnamon
Pinch sea salt, or to taste
¼ cup walnuts
1 cup pitted Medjool dates
2 tablespoons raisins
2 tablespoons sunflower seeds

Combine the almonds, cinnamon, and salt in the food processor and pulse into chunks. Add the walnuts and pulse into chunks. Add the dates, raisins, and sunflower seeds and pulse to mix well.

Scoop the dough by 1½ tablespoons onto a sheet tray lined with parchment and flatten into cookies.

Will keep for a week or more in your fridge or for several weeks in the freezer (thaw before eating).

*J*UST LIKE THE title says, these recipes are all very simple—simple to make, that is, but definitely not simple in flavor. Low in effort, they are huge in surprising new taste combinations like apples and rosemary, pineapple and ginger, salty watermelon, and mango and coconut with cayenne.

These surprising new tastes will elevate simple fruit to an elegant dessert for company or an anytime treat for family. They make it easy for us to bolster our intake of fresh, organic fruits that are chock-full of vitamins and minerals to help increase our overall health and well-being. They're full of fiber and water that fill us up and keep our sweet tooth feeling satisfied longer.

I always push for fresh and organic fruits whenever possible. Frozen fruits won't quite have the same texture or flavor as fresh, but you can also enjoy these recipes year-round by using frozen if you'd like. Enjoy your fruit simples immediately for the most distinctive taste and texture.

Fleur de Sel Kissed Watermelon

Fleur de sel is a sea salt harvested in France from salt ponds along the coast. Use your favorite sea salt here, the coarser the better. The salt crystals look pretty against the pink of the melon and accent its sweetness nicely.

Watermelon is a great source of beta-carotene and lycopene. It has 40 percent more lycopene than tomatoes and doesn't need cooking to unleash it.

8 slices watermelon, chilled
¼ teaspoon fleur de sel or coarse sea
    salt

Place the watermelon slices on a serving platter. Sprinkle lightly with sea salt and serve.

Best enjoyed immediately, but will keep in the fridge for a day.

Berries and Peaches with Almond Frangipane Kream

MAKES 4 SERVINGS

There's no better warm-weather treat than summer berries and sliced peaches topped with a rich almond kream. I love eating antioxidant-rich berries (even while picking them from the vine), and I'm lucky to have a friend with a peach tree who lets me pick all the peaches I can eat!

2 cups raspberries, blueberries, and/or
  blackberries (about 1 pint)
2 peaches, seeded and sliced
3 tablespoons agave syrup (optional)
Almond Frangipane Kream (page 169)

Combine the berries, peaches, and agave syrup (if using) in a mixing bowl and mix well. To serve, divide among 4 bowls and top with the kream.

Will keep for 1 day in the fridge. The kream will keep for several days in the fridge when stored separately.

Beauty-Boosting Vitamins A, C, and E

TO HELP YOUR skin build new skin cells and create more collagen, enjoy fruits with the three key beauty vitamins—A, C, and E—and reap the benefits of firm, glowing skin.

VITAMIN A protects our skin from sun damage and reduces production of the oil that causes blemishes. It is also needed for cell production and it regulates how fast skin cells grow and shed. It's a strong exfoliant, giving our skin a smoother, cleaner glow. To get more vitamin A into your diet, enjoy cantaloupe, mango, watermelon, and avocados.

VITAMIN C builds collagen (the protein in our skin that keeps it firm and youthful looking) and new skin tissue for plump skin that springs back. It helps heal wounds, decreases wrinkles, and neutralizes free-radical damage. Goji berries, acai, mango, citrus, plums, and berries are great sources of vitamin C.

VITAMIN E erases fine lines and repairs skin tissue and scarring. Find it in mango, blackberries, nuts, hemp oil, flax oil, and olives and olive oil. Healthy oils also keep your metabolism in check while acting as a natural skin lubricant to prevent premature signs of aging.

Sliced Apples with Rosemary

MAKES 4 SERVINGS

Simple crisp apple slices are sprinkled with touches of rosemary in this super-simple fall dessert. I prefer fresh rosemary when available. You can use dried here, but the flavor and color of fresh is more vibrant and fragrant.

2 apples, sliced
½ lemon
1 teaspoon chopped fresh rosemary, or
½ teaspoon chopped dried rosemary

Divide the apples among 4 dessert dishes and sprinkle with lemon juice. Top with pinches of rosemary and serve.

Best enjoyed immediately, but will keep for 1 day in the fridge.

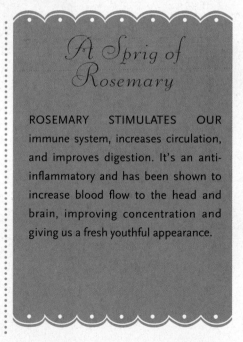

A Sprig of Rosemary

ROSEMARY STIMULATES OUR immune system, increases circulation, and improves digestion. It's an anti-inflammatory and has been shown to increase blood flow to the head and brain, improving concentration and giving us a fresh youthful appearance.

Pineapple with Ginger and Lime

MAKES 4 SERVINGS

Juicy pineapple slices are drizzled with sweet agave syrup and splashed with lime juice, then topped with fresh ginger. Both ginger and pineapple have anti-inflammatory properties to relieve sunburn and swelling and increase circulation.

½ ripe pineapple, peeled, cored, halved, and sliced
2 tablespoons agave syrup (optional)
2 tablespoons lime juice (from 1 lime)
2 tablespoons slivered fresh ginger

Place the sliced pineapple on a plate. Drizzle with the agave syrup (if using) and lime juice, sprinkle with the ginger, and serve.

Best when enjoyed immediately but will keep in the fridge for 1 day.

Kitchen Linens

BE GREEN BY using organic cotton, hemp, and bamboo kitchen towels, napkins, and tablecloths. And, when they get dirty, wait until you have a full load of kitchen linens before washing. I make sure to wash kitchen linens on their own to avoid cross contamination from my dirty gym socks and to avoid food and oil stains on my clothing. When washing, use toxin-free eco-detergent and wash with a lower temperature and shorter cycle to save energy.

Mango with Coconut Kream

MAKES 4 SERVINGS

This recipe is inspired by a Thai mango–sticky rice dessert. I like to top it off with a dash of cayenne pepper for the contrasting red and for a bit of heat. Hot peppers counteract inflammation and premature aging of the skin. Beta-carotene, which gives mangoes their color, is converted by our bodies into vitamin A, a well-known treatment for acne.

2 to 3 mangoes, peeled and diced
Coconut Kream (page 171)
Pinch of cayenne pepper (optional)

Toss the diced mango with half of the kream in a mixing bowl. Divide among 4 serving dishes and top each with 2 tablespoons of the kream. Sprinkle with cayenne, if desired, and serve.

Best enjoyed immediately but will keep for 1 day in fridge.

Toxin-Free Living

WHEN OUR BODIES are full of toxins and chemicals, disease sets in and aging speeds up. To look and feel your best, it's important to mind the toxins around you.

A clean, toxin-free home and work environment will help slow the aging process. Toxins are all around us, from the paint on our walls, to the cleansers in our bathrooms and kitchens, to our skin and hair products. Even our air and water are full of toxic poisons our bodies absorb. I can't always control the level of these poisons in all my environments, but I make sure not to bring additional toxic substances into my home.

By living cleaner and toxin-free, we're also living greener. By using toxin-free cleansers, paints, fabrics, and materials, we're supporting green businesses and decreasing the production and use of chemicals in our environment.

Researchers at the University of Washington found holiday baking and eating to have an environmental impact on Puget Sound. Treated sewage that went to the sound from the treatment plant showed cinnamon and vanilla levels rose between November 14 and December 9, with the largest spike right after Thanksgiving. In addition to benign substances showing up in our waters, prescription drugs, pesticides, chemicals like cleaners and perfumes, and even caffeine have been found to pass through the sewage system into public waterways. So, let's mind the products we use, how often we use them, and how we dispose of them.

8

Sun-Baked
Treats

*T*HE RECIPES IN this section use a dehydrator to dry food at a low temperature. I keep my heat below 104°F to make sure all enzymes stay alive and active so I get the most powerful nutritional benefits.

A dehydrator is a sun simulator, giving food a sun-dried effect. You can also place food directly in the sun to dry naturally in hotter months and in drier climates. Or, use your oven at the lowest temperature setting, propping open the door slightly to help lower the heat. Another option is to turn the oven on to warm slightly, then off to prevent overheating and leave the door closed. On again to heat, and off again, repeating as needed. As long as your hand isn't feeling too hot inside the oven, it's cool enough. Using your oven won't be efficient, takes more time, and may waste energy, but do the best you can. If you decide you like dehydrating, consider buying a dehydrator later.

Dry the recipes in this section to your liking. Shorter times mean more moisture and water and more enzyme activity, but a shorter shelf life. If planning to store food longer or at room temperature, dry it for a longer period of time, until all moisture has been removed. For toast or ice kream cones, the drier they are, the more crispy the texture will be.

Cranberry Scones

MAKES 2 DOZEN SCONES

These scones, with tart cranberries and raisins sprinkled in a moist almond and flaxseed dough, will quickly become your favorite. My secret ingredient is low-sugar, high-fiber carrot pulp for light sponginess. The scones keep well, travel with ease, and are packed with beautifying super-foods and nutrients like coconut oil, flaxseed, omega 3s and 6s, and beta-carotene.

3 cups applesauce (from 3 large apples; see "Carrot Pulp and Applesauce," page 148)

2 cups carrot pulp (from 4 to 5 large carrots; see "Carrot Pulp and Apple-sauce," page 148)

2 cups almond meal

2 cups raisins

1 cup fresh or dried cranberries

½ cup liquid coconut oil

¼ cup agave syrup

1 cup brown or tan flaxseed

1 cup filtered water

Combine the applesauce, carrot pulp, and almond meal in a large mixing bowl and mix well. Add the raisins, cranberries, coconut oil, and agave syrup and stir until mixed well.

Combine the flaxseed and water in the blender and blend until mixed well. Add to the applesauce mixture in the bowl and stir until well mixed.

On dehydrator trays lined with Teflex or ParaFlexx sheets or parchment paper, measure about ½ cup dough and form into a triangular scone shape. Repeat with the remaining dough. Dehydrate for 8 to 12 hours, until dry or to desired consistency. If you don't have a dehydrator, place the scones on a sheet tray and place in the oven at the lowest temperature for about 8 hours, monitoring the oven and turning the heat on and off so it doesn't get too hot to put your hand inside.

Will keep for a week or more in the fridge. The drier they are, the longer they'll keep.

SERVING SUGGESTION:
Enjoy with your favorite kream, jam, sauce, or **Miso Coconut Butter** (page 151)

Carrot Pulp and Applesauce

TO MAKE CARROT pulp, all you need to do is juice carrots and use what is left over. If you don't have a juicer, visit a local juice bar to order carrot juice and ask for the leftover pulp. The pulp gives my scones a lighter texture—using shredded carrots won't work the same way since they have more moisture and are a different texture from the dry pulp.

Applesauce is super easy to make: Just place cored apples (with skin on or peeled) into the food processor and puree. It's that simple.

ANI'S RAW FOOD DESSERTS

Breakfast Toast

These breakfast toasts are super tasty topped with slices of avocado and/or tomato. It's a great way to start each day with flax, which is packed with almost twice the omega-3 benefits as fish oil. Flax is wonderful for our skin, hair, and nails and helps combat heart disease and certain types of cancers. Omega-3s also help to elevate our mood, making us happy and healthy.

2¼ cups filtered water
1 cup whole flaxseed
1 cup buckwheat groats
¼ teaspoon sea salt
⅔ cup sesame seeds
½ cup raisins
⅓ cup goji berries

Combine the water, flaxseed, buckwheat, and salt in a mixing bowl and mix well. Add the sesame seeds, raisins, and goji berries and mix well. Set aside for 20 minutes, until the mixture becomes gelatinous from the flaxseed; this helps the ingredients bind together into a dough.

Evenly spread a layer of dough about ¼- to ⅓-inch thick onto a 14 by 14-inch dehydrator tray lined with a Teflex or ParaFlexx sheet or parchment paper. The dough should fill the entire tray. Dehydrate at 104°F for 3 to 4 hours, or until firm enough to flip over. Flip, peel off the paper, and score into nine slices to make it easy to break into straight lines later.

Dehydrate for 5 to 6 hours longer or until desired texture. The drier the toast is, the crispier the crust, the chewier the raisins, and the longer it will keep. If less dehydrated, it will be more pliable, and should be eaten within a few days.

When completely dry, the toast will keep for a couple weeks or more, as long as it stays dry. I like to store in a paper bag. When less dry, it will keep for a few days when stored in your refrigerator in a sealed container.

Persimmon Jam and Butter Toast

MAKES 4 SERVINGS

A sweet jam kissed with tart lemon zest combines with a savory butter to spread on crisp slices of Breakfast Toast. Persimmons are very high in iron, potassium, and antioxidants including vitamins A and C and beta-carotene.

JAM
- 1 ripe persimmon, peeled and quartered
- 1 teaspoon grated lemon zest
- 2 tablespoons agave syrup (optional)

MISO COCONUT BUTTER
- 2 tablespoons unpasteurized white miso
- 3 tablespoons soft but not liquid coconut oil

TOAST
- 4 slices **Breakfast Toast** (page 149)

To make the jam, pulse the persimmons, zest, and agave syrup (if using) in the Personal Blender or food processor into a jam texture.

To make the butter, use a fork to mix the miso and coconut oil to soft whipped butter texture in a small bowl.

To serve, butter each slice of toast and top with jam.

The jam will keep for a few days in the refrigerator. The butter will keep there for many weeks.

PB&J

Spread slices of Breakfast Toast with rich creamy nut butter and beautiful berry jam for a nostalgic lunch. Try heating up the toast with the nut butter in your dehydrator (before adding the jam) to recreate a modern version of warm toasted bread spread with melting peanut butter.

1½ cups strawberries, raspberries, blueberries, and/or blackberries
1 cup favorite raw nut butter, such as almond, cashew, or pecan
8 slices **Breakfast Toast** (page 149)

Smash the berries with a fork in a mixing bowl. You may want to keep some of the berries whole.

To serve, spread about 2 tablespoons nut butter onto each slice of toast. Spoon jam onto four of these slices. Top each jam slice with a non-jam slice. The assembled sandwiches are best eaten immediately.

The jam will keep for 2 days in the fridge. The nut butters will keep for months in the fridge.

Your Hat and Sunglasses

THIS CHAPTER MAY be about sun-baking our food, but by all means, we want to avoid baking our skin. Spending 20 to 30 minutes outside for a healthy dose of vitamin D is recommended by health experts—the amount of exposure depends on the time of year and climate, of course. But you want to avoid excessive exposure, which can lead to long-term skin damage, premature aging, and even skin cancer.

The sun generates both UVB and UVA rays. UVB rays are the "B"urning rays causing sunburns, and UVA rays are "A"ging rays, penetrating deep into our skin causing elasticin and collagen fibers to break down. Direct exposure to midday sun can lead to cumulative skin damage and leathery, tough-looking skin.

The ingredients in these recipes help protect and heal your skin from sun damage, but keep in mind the best protection is a hat, sunglasses, and avoiding the sun in the middle of the day.

Strawberry Macaroons

MAKES 6 SERVINGS

A light, spongy blend of strawberries and coconut creates a taste reminiscent of strawberry jam. Rich coconut and antioxidant-packed strawberries give us that glow of healthy radiance.

1 cup fresh or frozen strawberries
⅓ cup pitted Medjool dates
⅓ cup agave syrup
1 tablespoon alcohol-free vanilla extract, or the seeds from 1 vanilla bean
2 cups shredded coconut

Combine the strawberries, dates, agave syrup, and vanilla in the food processor and mix well. Add the coconut and pulse to mix.

Use a 2-tablespoon scooper or your hands to roll the dough into balls. Place on dehydrator trays, no parchment or Teflex needed, and dehydrate at 104°F for 3 to 6 hours, as desired. Note: These macaroons will remain spongy even when completely dry.

Will keep for a week or more in the refrigerator.

Candied Citrus Zest

MAKES 6 TO 8 SERVINGS

Candied zest is **a fun way to add a splash of color and beauty to any dish. By dipping strips of zest in a little bit of agave syrup and then dehydrating them, you retain the zest's vibrant color, but it will remain a bit sticky, even when dry.**

2 tablespoons agave syrup
2 tablespoons filtered water
2 oranges, limes, and/or lemons

Mix the agave syrup and water in a small bowl. Use the citrus zester to zest long strips of peel from the citrus fruits. Dip the zest in the agave syrup mixture and place on the dehydrator tray lined with a Teflex or ParaFlexx sheet or parchment paper. Dehydrate at 104°F for 6 hours or longer, or until desired texture.

VARIATION:
Dehydrate zest strips without agave syrup for 2 to 4 hours, or until crisp. The color will be less vibrant, but the zest will be crispier and drier. To make long skinny spirals, wrap long strips of zest along the length of a chopstick and dry in the dehydrator.

Banana Bread Biscuits

MAKES 12 BISCUITS

Yes, it's true—you can have living foods biscuits! This is a deliciously nutritious banana bread with maple-flavored pecans and sweet cashews. Bananas are high in potassium, which has been shown to increase our levels of serotonin to elevate our mood. Banana bread is good mood food!

2 cup dry cashews
¼ teaspoon salt
2 ripe bananas
1 teaspoon alcohol-free vanilla extract
½ cup dry pecans, chopped

Combine the cashews and salt in the food processor and process into small pieces. Break up the bananas and add to the processor with the vanilla. Process to mix well. Add the pecans and pulse to mix.

Use a 1½-tablespoon scooper or a spoon to drop batter into rounds onto dehydrator trays. Dehydrate at 104°F for 6 to 8 hours, or until desired consistency.

Will keep for several days or longer in the fridge. The drier the biscuits, the longer they will keep.

Skin Care Recipe:
Banana Wrap for Moist Silky Skin

 BIOTIN IS THE most important B vitamin for our skin. It forms the basis of skin, nail, and hair cells and gives skin a healthy glow while hydrating cells and increasing overall skin tone. Bananas are a great source of both biotin and potassium, which helps us maintain healthy, beautiful skin and hair, is great for wrinkles, and plumps up our skin.

1 very ripe banana
2 tablespoons olive oil

Mash the banana with a fork in a small bowl. Add the oil and mix well.

Fill a mixing bowl with very warm filtered water. Place a face towel in the water.

Spread the banana mixture onto your face and neck. Cover with paper or tissue, and top with the warm damp towel. Relax on the bed or couch for 20 to 30 minutes. Shower with warm water to remove.

Blueberry Muffins with Lemon Blackberry Glaze

MAKES 6 MUFFINS

These muffins are like blueberry biscuits served in a cupcake cup. They're moist, delicious, and look pretty with violet-colored glaze. Full of omega-3s and 6s, antioxidants, and vitamins, they're great in the morning with a cup of tea, juice, or smoothie.

MUFFINS
- 1⅔ cups almond meal
- 1 cup golden flax meal (about ¾ cup whole seeds ground into powder)
- ¼ teaspoon sea salt
- 2 tablespoons agave syrup
- 1 tablespoon alcohol-free vanilla extract, or the seeds from 1 vanilla bean
- 1 tablespoon liquid coconut oil
- ⅓ cup filtered water, as needed
- 1½ cups fresh or frozen blueberries

GLAZE
- ½ cup cashews, ground into a fine powder
- 2 tablespoons blackberry juice (from about ⅓ cup blackberries pushed through a wire sieve)
- 2 tablespoons lemon juice (from about ½ lemon)
- 2 tablespoons agave syrup
- 1 tablespoon filtered water, as needed

To make the muffins, mix together the almond meal, flax meal, and salt in a mixing bowl. Add the agave syrup, vanilla, and coconut oil and mix well. Add the water and mix to a batter consistency. Fold in the blueberries.

Place 6 cupcake liners into a muffin pan and spoon about ½ cup dough into each. Place the pan in the dehydrator and dehydrate at 104°F for 4 to 6 hours, until the batter is dry and to desired consistency.

To make the glaze, combine the cashews, blackberry juice, lemon juice, agave syrup, and water in the Personal Blender with the 1-cup container and blend until smooth.

To serve, frost each muffin with the glaze.

Will keep for several days refrigerated. Can be frozen for several weeks and thawed. Warm muffins in the dehydrator at 104°F for an hour or two before serving.

Avoid Toxic Cleansers

INSTEAD OF USING toxic chlorine bleach, which washes up in our waterways and environment, give oxygen bleach a try for removing difficult stains.

Here's a trick used in hospitals to remove blood: Pour hydrogen peroxide over blood on fabric before it dries, and watch it disappear!

To disinfect, clean with hot water and soap. Or, mix 1/2 cup of borax with 1 gallon of hot water to disinfect and deodorize. Rubbing alcohol works great for disinfecting, too.

Avoid chlorine bleaches that are added to dishwashing detergents by choosing a nontoxic, green, eco-friendly detergent.

Ice Kream Cones

Thin light wafers **are rolled up into cones and dried until crispy and flaky. They are delicious as holders for ice kream and sorbet, or crumbled to top kreams and desserts. I use pre-sprouted and ground flax powder from Navitas Naturals.**

1 cup filtered water
⅓ cup chopped cored apple (about ½ small apple)
1 tablespoon firmly packed pitted Medjool dates
½ cup ground tan flaxseed
⅓ cup ground buckwheat groats

Combine the water, apple, and dates in the blender and blend until smooth. Transfer to a mixing bowl. Add the flaxseed powder and buckwheat powder. Use a spoon or a whisk to stir and mix well.

Scoop the batter onto a 14 by 14-inch dehydrator tray lined with a Teflex or ParaFlexx sheet or parchment paper. Spread into an even layer about ⅛-inch thick. The batter should fill the entire tray. Place in the dehydrator and dry at 104°F for 3 to 4 hours, or until dry enough to flip.

Carefully flip the crust, and then gently peel off the paper. Using a butter knife, score one direction in half, and then score the other direction into thirds to make a total of 6 rectangles.

To make cones, carefully roll each rectangle into a cone shape, about 4 inches high with the opening about 2 inches in diameter. (This is the perfect size to hold two 1½-tablespoon scoops of ice kream.) Place the cones on the dehydrator tray and dehydrate at 104°F for 2 to 3 hours longer, until dry and crisp. Check each hour to make sure no cones have collapsed. If so, rotate the cone, or use a bent paperclip to keep the opening round.

Will keep for many weeks in freezer.

SERVING SUGGESTION:
Use cones to make **Sundae Cones** (page 37).

9

Sauces
and
Kreams

*N*O MATTER IF you're home alone and want a simple, elegant treat or are making desserts for guests, one simple way to add complexity to any dish is with a sauce. All of the following sauces and kreams can be added to desserts to add extra dimensions of flavor, texture, and color. Make extra so you always have some on hand to dress up any sweet snack. Indeed, the recipes are so easy, it won't matter much if you're making a sauce or kream for one person or for fifty.

How easy? Simply whip up lavender flowers and agave syrup to make a light, aromatic Lavender Syrup; make decadent Chocolate Sauce by blending cacao powder and agave syrup with a splash of olive oil; and blend together almonds, vanilla, and agave syrup to make a rich Almond Frangipane Kream.

You don't even need a blender to make Acai Sauce or Cinnamon Sauce. Just combine acai, or cinnamon and spices, with agave syrup in a jar and shake to mix.

Most of the recipes make smaller ½ to 1-cup batches, so you'll want to use your Personal Blender if blending. If you're using a larger blender, double or triple the recipe so there's enough liquid to cover the blender blades. All my sauces can be frozen for several weeks or more and thawed before using.

Almond Frangipane Kream

MAKES 1½ CUPS

Frangipane typically refers to an almond-flavored pastry cream. My delicious sweet almond kream has a touch of vanilla and would be a yummy addition to pretty much all of the desserts in this book. Make a couple batches so you'll always have some on hand to enjoy with fresh-cut fruits, cakes, and cobblers. The kream is also great taking the lead as a pudding when topped with fresh berries.

1 cup almonds
1 cup filtered water
2 tablespoons agave syrup
1 tablespoon alcohol-free vanilla, or the
    seeds from 1 vanilla bean

Combine all the ingredients in the high-speed blender and blend until smooth, at least 30 seconds.

Will keep for 3 to 4 days in the fridge or several weeks in the freezer (thaw and stir before using).

Coconut Kream

This is a white, **sweet, rich kream full of coconut flavor that's great for topping desserts and fresh fruit.**

¾ cup shredded coconut, ground into powder
¾ cup cashews, ground into powder
¾ cup filtered water
¼ cup + 2 tablespoons liquid coconut oil
¼ cup + 1 tablespoon agave syrup

Place all the ingredients in the Personal Blender with the 1-cup container and blend until mixed well.

Will keep in the fridge for a week or more or for several weeks in the freezer (thaw before using).

Lavender Syrup

MAKES ½ CUP

Lavender is beautiful in color, has an amazing floral scent, and is known for many medicinal properties, including relaxation. Serve this syrup with muffins and cookies, on ice kream, or as a dip for fruit. What a delicious way to relax!

    2 tablespoons fresh lavender flowers or
        1 tablespoon dried
    ½ cup agave syrup

Combine the ingredients in the Personal Blender with the 1-cup container and blend for at least 30 seconds or longer, until mixed well. Monitor to make sure the syrup doesn't get too hot in the blender.

Will keep for several days in the fridge or for weeks in the freezer (thaw before using).

Cinnamon Sauce

MAKES ½ CUP

Drizzle this clear, spicy, sweet sauce over cake, cobblers, ice kream, and any other favorite desserts.

    ½ cup agave syrup
    ½ teaspoon alcohol-free vanilla extract
    ½ teaspoon ground cinnamon
    ¼ teaspoon ground nutmeg

Combine all the ingredients in a small jar with a lid. Cover tightly and shake to mix well.

Will keep for many weeks in the fridge or freezer (thaw before using).

Feed Your Skin a Fruit Salad

PINEAPPLE IS DELICIOUS in many raw desserts. But did you know that it's super beneficial for your skin too? Pineapple has anti-inflammatory properties, is a mild astringent, and its enzymes dissolve skin's dead cells and dirt. It's a great component of this fruit salad skin mask, which also includes bananas to make our skin smooth and soft; kiwi, which is high in vitamin C and enzymes; and honeydew melon to cool and hydrate. If you have fruit that's too ripe to eat, try making this salad for your skin. Apply the mask pool or ocean-side—it's sticky and fun.

2 cups chopped peeled pineapple
2 cups chopped honeydew melon
1 banana, chopped
2 kiwi fruit, peeled and chopped

Combine all the ingredients in the food processor and process into a lumpy texture. Apply to body and face and leave on for 20 to 30 minutes. Rinse in an outdoor shower, with a hose, or in the ocean and enjoy smooth radiant skin!

Pineapple Sauce

MAKES 1 CUP

This sweet chunky syrup is perfect for topping ice kream, banana splits, and other favorite sweet treats. Known as nature's healing fruit, pineapple is high in vitamin C and also contains bromelain, a natural anti-inflammatory that helps relieve stress.

1½ cups fresh or frozen pineapple
2 tablespoons agave syrup

Combine the ingredients in the Personal Blender with the 1-cup container and pulse to mix into a chunky sauce.

Will keep for 3 days in the fridge or for weeks in the freezer (thaw before using).

SERVING SUGGESTIONS:
Enjoy with fruits, other sauces, ice kreams, cakes, and cobblers. Try it as a delicious jam on **Breakfast Toast** (page 149) and in a PB&J (page 153).

Raspberry Sauce

This bright red sauce is a beautiful complement to ice kream sundaes and chocolate sweet treats.

½ cup fresh or frozen raspberries
¼ cup pitted semi-soft Medjool dates
¼ cup agave syrup
¼ cup filtered water

SERVING SUGGESTION:

Raspberry sauce is great as a filling for **Filled Chocolate Truffles** (page 89).

Combine all the ingredients in the Personal Blender with the 1-cup container and blend well.

Will keep for 3 days in the refrigerator or a few weeks in the freezer (thaw before using).

Acai Sauce

MAKES 1 CUP

I love acai for the flavor, beautiful purple color, and antioxidant blast. Somewhere between chocolate and red wine, the flavor is a great addition to any dessert or ice kream to add another layer of flavor complexity.

2 packages (100 grams each) frozen
    acai smoothie packs, thawed until
    liquid
¼ cup agave syrup

Combine the ingredients in a small jar with a lid. Cover tightly and shake to mix well. Or whisk in a small bowl to mix well.

Use immediately for maximum antioxidant benefits.

Chocolate Sauce

MAKES ABOUT 1/2 CUP

Here's a yummy, kreamy, decadent chocolate sauce for when you want to boost a treat with a bit of real chocolate zip. Use as a glaze, or chill to thicken and use as frosting. Or try swirling into ice kream or sorbet just before it freezes completely. The sauce doesn't freeze and stays gooey when cold.

½ cup cacao powder
½ cup agave syrup
1 tablespoon olive oil

Combine all the ingredients in the Personal Blender with the 1-cup container and blend or stir in a mixing bowl to mix well.

Will keep for several weeks in the fridge or even longer in the freezer (thaw before using).

10

Sparkling Desserts

with Wine and Champagne

WHEN SOME PEOPLE think of raw foods and a healthy lifestyle, they think it needs to be an all-or-nothing approach. Some may exclude alcohol. I say moderation is key. Studies have shown numerous benefits of the antioxidant and anti-inflammatory properties in white, red, and sparkling wines, including anti-aging benefits, lung and heart health boosters; prevention of ulcers, cancer, and stroke; plus increases in bone strength (valuable for us women). The catch here is moderation: enjoying a glass of wine or champagne a day, and no more.

Extremes of any sort are never good for us, neither are all-or-nothing attitudes. Instead, it's important that we do the best we can every day and do better each day than the day before. Be patient and forgiving, changes don't need to happen overnight. After all, we've been accustomed to doing things a certain way our whole lives, so remember to allow time for change to happen. Love and forgive ourselves and others for not being perfect and get back on the horse after we fall off, rather than giving up completely. Health and well-being are life-long pursuits.

I choose organic wine and champagne, for both drinking and using in desserts, to avoid added sulfites used as preservatives. And yes, wine and champagne are both considered raw, unlike beer and spirits, which are distilled. Maximize your water intake and moderate your alcohol. Lots of water will help keep your skin hydrated, while alcohol in excess of one glass a day will dry it out.

Summer Fruit Salad in Herbed White Wine

MAKES 4 SERVINGS

What's more summery than stone fruits tossed in white wine and served for Sunday brunch in the garden? The surprise ingredient of rosemary helps brighten the flavors of the fruit and adds a freshness to the vanilla-and cinnamon-infused white wine.

HERBED WINE

1 cup dry white wine

¼ cup agave syrup

Seeds from 1 vanilla bean, or 1 tablespoon alcohol-free vanilla extract

¼ teaspoon chopped fresh rosemary or
dried rosemary

Pinch of cinnamon

FRUIT SALAD

1 nectarine, pitted and sliced

1 peach, pitted and sliced

2 apricots, pitted and sliced

4 pitted fresh figs, quartered

½ cup cherries, left whole

To make the herbed wine, combine the wine, agave syrup, vanilla, rosemary, and cinnamon in a small mixing bowl and mix well.

To make the salad, combine the nectarine, peach, apricots, figs, and cherries in a medium mixing bowl.

Drizzle the wine mixture over the fruit and serve. Best enjoyed immediately. Remember to watch for cherry pits.

Organic Biodynamic Wine

ORGANIC WINE IS made from organically grown grapes and *without* any additives like sulfites or tartaric acid. On the other hand, wines made with organic grapes that *do* have added sulfites or additives are labeled "Made with organically grown grapes."

Organic grapes are cultivated using cover crops and natural fertilizers instead of poisonous chemical fertilizers, herbicides, and insecticides. Organic farmers allow plants other than vines to grow in and around the vineyard, promoting biodiversity. This attracts good bugs that eat the bad ones, for example.

Many wines are made using animal products during processing. Bones, milk proteins, egg albumin, and dried blood powder are some of the ingredients used to clarify and clear wine of solid impurities like grape skins and stems and to adjust tannin levels in certain wines after fermentation. To find out which brands of wine are vegan, research online or contact a winemaker directly to ask.

Blueberries in Muscat Wine

with Coconut Ice Kream

MAKES 4 SERVINGS

Beautiful blueberries kissed **with sweet, floral muscat wine are a delicious way to get more of blueberries' vitamins, minerals, and antioxidant goodness into our bodies. This is a light, refreshing treat in the hot months when fresh berries are abundantly in season.**

> 1 pint blueberries
> 1 cup muscat or other flavorful dessert
>   wine
> **Coconut Ice Kream** (page 35)
> Fresh mint sprigs, for garnish

Divide the blueberries among 4 serving bowls or glasses. Drizzle with the wine, top with a scoop of ice kream, and garnish with mint. Enjoy immediately.

Strawberries in

Champagne

MAKES 4 SERVINGS

Enjoying delicious fresh **strawberries is a simple way to add bright red color, antioxidants, good-for-you vitamins and minerals, and more complex flavor to your diet. Feel free to substitute your favorite berries for the strawberries here and to even muddle them by crushing in your bowl. This is worth celebrating.**

> 1 pint strawberries, sliced
> 3 tablespoons agave syrup
> 1 cup champagne or sparkling wine
> 2 teaspoons grated lemon zest
> Fresh mint sprigs, for garnish

Divide the strawberries among 4 serving bowls. Drizzle with the agave syrup, then the champagne. Sprinkle on the zest and garnish with a sprig of mint. Best enjoyed immediately.

Eco-Entertaining

CONSIDER OUR ENVIRONMENT when planning your next soirée. You may be pleasantly surprised to discover it can save you money to be green.

SEND DIGITAL INVITATIONS

Email is a convenient way to invite friends to an event. You can even create your own invitation card, scan it into your computer, and attached it to the email invite. It's always nice to follow up with a phone call, too. For traditional snail-mail invites, choose postconsumer recycled paper and soy ink if possible.

USE YOUR OWN PLATES, CUPS, AND SERVINGWARE

Always use real silverware, glasses, and dishes if possible. Give your caterer your own serving dishes to use to avoid ugly, cheap-looking disposable platters. A bit Bohemian, but I've been known to asked friends to bring their own plate, bowl, and cutlery. For large groups, look for recycled plastic. Better yet, seek out corn or potato-based plastic cutlery and plates, which break down in about three months. Bamboo's a great option as well—it's renewable and biodegradable.

RENT, DON'T BUY

It's surprisingly cost-effective to rent tables and chairs from a local party rental store, rather than buying your own. Most even rent tablecloths and glasses, which you return dirty, so they do the washing!

GREEN DÉCOR

Decorate with locally grown flowers or potted plants that you can give away as party favors afterwards. Consider a centerpiece made with fruits and vegetables or try arranging beautiful fresh fruits like berries and figs as a runner down the center of the table. Dim the lights and use soy candles.

BE THRIFTY

Score at your local thrift store or flea market on cloth napkins, place mats, serving bowls, pie and casserole dishes, plates, and glasses. Bandanas make good cheap napkins.

RECYCLE AND COMPOST

Make it easy for guests to recycle and compost by placing separate bins near the garbage cans. This will save you from having to pick through to separate out recyclables later. I save glass bottles, peel off the labels, and use them as vases.

CONSIDER TRANSPORTATION

Pick a location that's easy to get to with public transit or help friends set up ride shares.

CHOOSE LOCAL, SEASONAL, ORGANIC

Shop at your farmers' market for bulk seasonal ingredients at lower prices than you'll find at a grocery store. Consider asking people to bring a bottle of organic wine to help offset your party budget.

CLEAN UP GREEN

Cut up and use old towels for mopping and cleaning. Old t-shirts cut into ¼-panel squares make great dusting cloths. If using cleansers, make sure they are nontoxic and environmentally friendly. Don't bother to pre-rinse dishes before putting them in the dishwasher, and make sure it is full before you run it.

Prunes Poached in Red Wine and Rosemary

MAKES 4 SERVINGS

Give prunes a try with this beautiful, richly colored, antioxidant-packed treat. Prunes are high in potassium and beta-carotene to protect us from cell damage, cancer, and heart disease. Their soluble fiber normalizes blood sugar levels and helps prevent and treat Type 2 diabetes. Prunes also reduce inflammation and cholesterol and give us a sense of fullness to prevent overeating and help us lose weight.

1½ cups dry red wine
¼ cup agave syrup
1 tablespoon lemon zest
½ teaspoon chopped fresh rosemary or
 ¼ teaspoon dried
1 cup prunes
2 tablespoons chopped almonds, for
 garnish

Combine the wine, agave syrup, lemon zest, and rosemary in a small mixing bowl and mix well. Add the prunes and soak for at least 1 hour before serving.

To serve, divide among 4 serving bowls or stemware and top with the chopped almonds.

Will keep for 1 day in the fridge.

Apricots in Spiced White Wine Syrup

MAKES 4 SERVINGS

This spiced dessert gives me a nostalgic feeling of autumn, with the changing color of the leaves and the pumpkins and festive Halloween decorations. Its antioxidants and rich nutrients will help beautify even the scariest of goons and goblins. As with all recipes, feel free to substitute your favorite fresh and dried fruits for the dried apricots. Most will taste great with the Indian-inspired flavor of fennel seeds, cinnamon, cloves, and black pepper.

1 cup dry white wine
¼ cup agave syrup
1 tablespoon lemon zest
½ teaspoon fennel seeds
Pinch of ground cinnamon
Pinch of ground cloves
Pinch of black pepper
1 cup dried apricots

Combine the wine, agave syrup, lemon zest, fennel seeds, cinnamon, cloves, and pepper in a mixing bowl and mix well. Add the apricots and soak for at least 15 minutes before serving.

Will keep in the fridge for a couple days.

SERVING SUGGESTION:

In a bowl or glass, place a scoop or two of **Coconut Ice Kream** (page 35), top with soaked apricots, and drizzle with wine syrup.

Metabolic Boosters for a Trimmer You

ANY FOOD IN excess won't do us any good. Especially alcohol. Overindulging can cause weight gain, acne and dry skin, and sleep problems—and also jeopardize healthy eating habits. Remember to practice moderation and include more whole fresh foods in your diet. Here are some more of my keys to good living:

EAT OFTEN Our metabolism speeds up when we eat. Burn more calories by snacking frequently on my healthy treats and nutrient-rich, disease-fighting, beautifying, slimming superfoods like fresh fruits, veggies, nuts, and seeds.

BUILD MUSCLE The more muscle we have, the higher our metabolism runs, and the more calories we burn. Do push-ups and sit-ups, use resistance bands, or lift light weights and build more muscle while increasing bone density and combating osteoporosis.

SWEAT Walk briskly, jog, swim, hike, and bike. Aerobic activity is important for sweating out toxins, increasing circulation, burning calories, and boosting metabolism.

SLEEP Chill out and catch more zzzz's. Relax, lower your cortisol levels, burn more fat, and boost your metabolism.

DRINK WATER Drink half your body weight in ounces of filtered water daily to keep yourself hydrated, clean, and feeling full.

CHOOSE VEGAN Avoid foods that make you swell, bloat, and break out with acne like meats, eggs, and dairy.

Thanks

JAE PHYO, MY mother, thank you for a lifetime of inspiration for living healthy, treading lightly on our planet, eating green and raw, and for being kind, loving, compassionate, and radiantly gorgeous.

Max Phyo, my amazing brother, thank you for helping me out of many binds, for your valuable legal advice, for your Hollywood hookups, and for being my biggest fan. You're my hero.

Dr. Ruben Cartegena: Thank you for believing in me, for our nutrition and medical discussions, and your valuable consulting and help.

A very special thank you to Seth Beck and John Beck for the artist-in-residency at the Beck School of Architecture and Design. Thank you Seth for your beautiful photos in this book. Thank you John for letting me take over your refrigerators and test kitchens for weeks at a time. Paulette, Jessie, Sarah, Stuart, and Keri: Thanks for being my taste testers and advocates.

Antonio Sanchez, my star illustrator: Thanks for creating the gorgeous icons in this book.

Duc Nguyen: Thank you for your beautiful ingredient photos.

Dora Jih, Sam Schiff, tri-athletes and Iron-men, thanks for inviting me into your travel test kitchen, for your love and support, and kick-butt spinning classes.

Thanks Ava and Ana for your help in the kitchen as my extra sets of mini 4- and 6-year-old hands and taste testers, and Aiden for being my youngest book promoter.

Ana Sage, thanks for your check-ins, visits to the sauna, massages, scrumptious food, recipe testing, and tasting. You mean so much to me. Chef Ito, thank you for many energizing, love-filled meals, and your contagious zest for life. Dan Mapes, thank you for your encouragement, love, support, gentle nudges, and words of wisdom over the past 15 years. Linda Devers, you're an angel sent from above, thank you for taking a big load off my plate so I could stay focused on writing my book.

Ede Schweizer: Thank you, I wouldn't be here today without your support and inspiration over the past decade. My good friends and fellow authors Brendan Brazier, Matt Amsden, and Bryant Terry: Thank you for being my support group. You're inspira-tional, and it's awesome that we get to build our future together . . . even on the same writing schedules!

Wes Crain, Zach Adelman, and Jill Morgyn at Navitas Naturals, Jae Kyoung Choi, Brian Choi, and Mia Lunasco at Tribest Corporation, John Roulac at Nutiva, and Kaia Lai and Jeremy Black at Sambazon: Thank you for making my favorite products and for your contributions in creating social equality while building a green sustainable planet for us all.

Thanks to my editor, Renee Sedliar, for believing in my vision and this book, and Wendie Carr, my publicist, for your excitement and creativity.

Thank you Bill Ahmann and Perkins Coie for believing in me and for the future we're building together. I can't thank you enough for your valuable insight and advice Bill, and for your help reclaiming my brand.

Index

INDEX